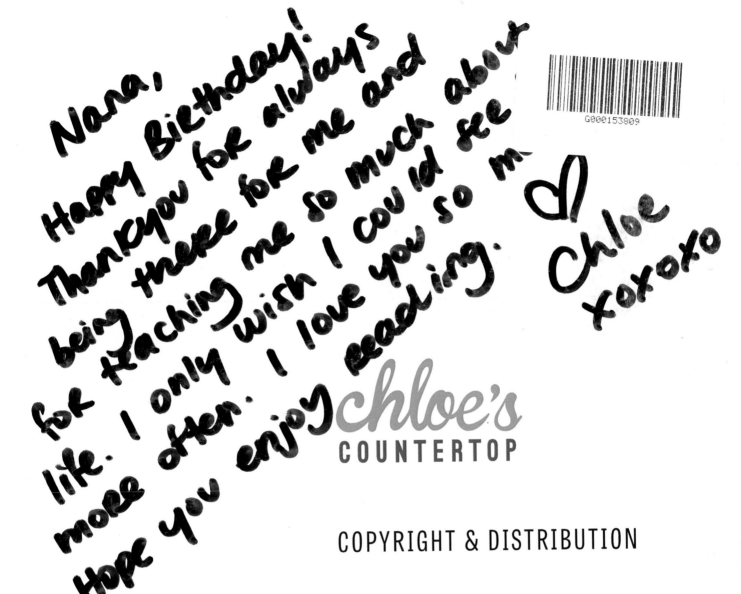

Nana,
Happy Birthday!
Thankyou for always
there for me and
being there for me and
for Reaching me so much about
life. I only wish I cou'ld see
more often. I love you so m—
Hope you enjoy reading.

♡ Chloe
xoxoxo

chloe's
COUNTERTOP

COPYRIGHT & DISTRIBUTION

Portrait Photos by:

©Mary Beth Koeth

©The Essence Oracle

©Alyson Strike

©Stephanie Hamilton

"

*Why do you stay in prison when
the door is wide open?*

—Rumi

"

The living, loving, and learning never ends.

Just when you think that you're finished and it's over; you lie, flat on your beautiful ass, on the ground, in complete humility.

Because you are here, and you are human.

I thought I was done. I thought I was recovered. I thought I was perfect. I thought I had reached my destination.

And then I realised- thank goodness I haven't.

Let's lose control.
Let's let go of the past.
Let's stop planning for the future.
Let's be here. Now. Together.
I've got you.

- Chloe

FORWARD

Living in Light is the one book I share with any female who's struggling with a tumultuous relationship to food and their ever-changing body image.

As a college student, I was in therapy for an eating disorder. To try and compensate for the extreme challenges I had with food and body image, I collected every trendy cookbook and diet and immersed myself into a new world of more restriction—things I wasn't allowed to eat anymore, exercises I was not doing enough of. I enabled my already defunct eating and guilt-driven exercising habits by adding more rules into the mix. I was not making choices intuitively, but instead, out of guilt. Which made me feel like I was stuck in a hamster wheel of choices that never felt right.

If I wasn't seeing results, it must have been that at some point, I missed a rule in one of the many diet books that took up most of the shelf space in my library. "It must be me, I've fallen off the wagon. I could have done better." Surely the books I was devouring weren't false. They were published with strong testimonials from other people who said the process worked.

It had to be me that needed fixing, not the diet trends or extreme exercises. I was in such dire need of the right advice.

I am lucky enough to have finally got it right, and man does it feel liberating to live without worry I'm eating the wrong thing or not doing the right exercise. The intuitive principles of Living in Light are the reasons I was able to stop spending countless days and months, wasted, scouring over trendy diet books and workouts.

When I finally found the lifestyle choices that felt divine to me, it did not involve massive restrictions; this is when I knew it was a lifestyle I could stick with. The philosophy that Chloe offers in Living in Light actually works.

As it turns out, the whole truth, about food and body image, is much more simple than we make it out to be. We knew this as we came into our Earth Suits and then learned otherwise over the accumulated years of society's changing beauty ideals and nutrition fads. Our body knew what we needed from day one, we have to remember that again.

It's vital that we forget what we've learned over the years, unlearn what is untrue, and remember what we've known from the very beginning: how to eat from Mother Earth, move to feel good, make decisions that feel divine to us, and how to see our bodies in each other and in nature.

Chloe offers her experiential wisdom as a learning tool for rapid awareness and as a refresher for the times we need a beautiful reminder. In Living in Light, Chloe takes us through the entire process of consumption and self-love in a way that makes us question, "seriously, it's that easy?"

Thank you, Chloe, for putting into words what I know will benefit all who enjoy your transformational labor of love.

Ajo,

Emily Nolan

Chief Empowerment Officer, Emilynolan.com

A NOTE FROM CHLOE

It's taken some time to get this book out. It's been brewing for several years, and is a true reflection of my conscious living journey. I wouldn't be here without the beautiful Chloe's Countertop community and followers. This book is dedicated to you. May you find yourself in my stories, inspiration in my recipes, joy in my photos and true health in your kitchen. Be patient with yourself. Creation and balance takes time and the journey is most definitely more important than the destination. You are loved.

To my family- thank you for offering me gifts that I only began to appreciate and understand lately.

Friends- thank you for always being there, loving me, supporting me, reading my work over and over and being my biggest fans. You know who you are and I love you.

To my brand and design team- you guys are incredible. Thank you so much for all of your hard work, dedication and patience with this project. I am so grateful to have you in my life and I hope that you feel as proud as I do to have this out in the universe.

XO

P.S. Faris, you are loved too. Thank you for recipe testing, editing, reading, eating, and loving. Thank you for being there.

CONTENTS

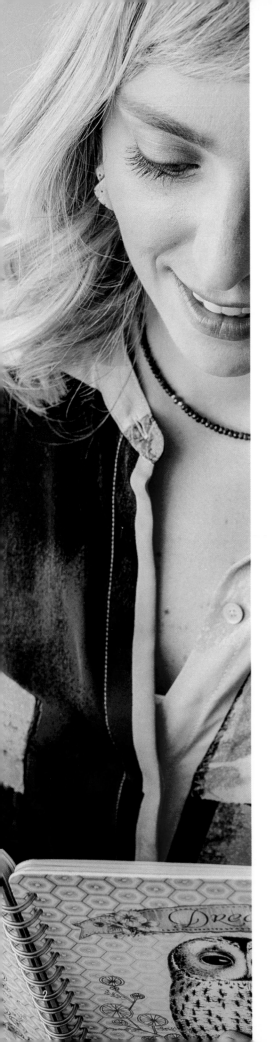

We all have a food story. No matter who you are, ever since you entered this world food has been a part of your life. For most of us, food has shown up at least 3 times a day, every single day since birth. Food stimulates emotion. Food represents memories. Food is fundamental to life.

For me, food wasn't always a happy part of life. Food represented loss of control, anxiety, fear and worthlessness. Instead of allowing food to nourish, energize and support me- I obsessed about it, focused on it and attached all of my value to it. You have a food story as well. Maybe it's a happy story. Maybe it's about physical pain. Perhaps it sounds a lot like mine. Our stories are a part of what connects us; they are what make us human. And here you are. It's time to release your food story, let go of control- and allow food to truly nourish and support you. You're ready to change your relationship with food and your body, and to allow the gifts of Mother Nature to be what they are- gifts.

In this book you will find all of Chloe's tips, tricks, and magical secrets to living consciously and eating intuitively. Inside is a careful collection of everything you need to know to uncover your truth, discover balance and cook and eat in love- like you never have before. I hope this book offers you the support you need, brings magic into your life and inspires you to love food, your body and most importantly- to love you.

chloe's
COUNTERTOP

REACH OUT

If you do re-create my recipes, follow my guides and use my tricks, please do share them with me:

www

www.chloescountertop.com

✉

info@chloescountertop.com

@chloescountertop

🐦

@chloecountertop

#

#chloescountertop

INTRODUCTION

The truth is, I've written this introduction about thirty times over. Writing an introduction to your first book is almost as challenging as figuring out the perfect elevator pitch. It's not easy. Where do you start and what do you include? I want to tell you everything. So here it goes, my attempt at the thirty-first introduction for my book. Here goes my im-perfect elevator pitch.

Welcome to Chloe's Countertop, the book (so far, good start).

It honestly humbles me beyond that you're reading this and that you have offered me the opportunity to enter your life and share my story with you. It is such a pleasure and I hope this book begins to express my immense gratitude for being here with you.

My story begins from the moment courage took the front seat.

I spent a lot of life envisioning what I wanted for myself. I always remember looking around, seeing all these talented people- and dreaming of it. Dreaming that I could be on a stage, doing gymnastics with Cirque Du Soleil, juggling or performing an inspiring act of beauty. I wished I were a ballerina, or a dancer on Broadway. I remember going to shows and feeling so intensely in awe at the end, during standing ovation. I had a deep desire to feel what they were feeling- loved, valued... worthy.

I always wished for something that would allow me to stand out- to be seen, to be special. All the while, I spent my time looking outside of myself, wishing for something more. I wanted to be better. I was very much in the space of "I am not good enough" and "I need to change". It wasn't until I found Holistic Nutrition that things began to shift.

66

Once you begin to do this work and practice awareness in your life, things that once had power no longer contain the same charge.

Suddenly, I discovered a passion. I was always good at things, I excelled at almost everything I did- but passion was missing. My passion was more for excelling and less for actually doing. The issue with this is that being good at something, or excelling- is not sustainable. You cannot build a life of happiness on something, just because you are good at it. There has to be more. There has to be passion.

Since I became a Holistic Nutritionist I have noticed such a massive shift in regards to the amount of people dedicating their lives to finding passion and discovering truth. So many people are what we now call a 'foodie'. In fact, a foodie is actually a genuine and successful career now. On the one hand, this is fantastic- people are being celebrated for choosing to live their lives in passion. On the other hand- it is difficult because more and more people are saturating this food-filled market. Foodies are everywhere. No matter where you go in the world- chances are you will see someone snapping their food near by. It used to be almost impossible for a strict-vegan to travel and sustain themselves on the local food culture. Now, it is more or less becoming the norm. Menus have gluten-free, nut-free, paleo, refined-sugar free, organic and vegan options. Plants are being celebrated. Sustainability is becoming the norm. So many wonderful things are happening in this foodie community.

One of the downfalls with saturation: people get lost. Lost in comparison, lost in judgment and lost in fear. With saturation comes competition and suddenly, you are no longer the only one not only good at what you are doing, but loving what you are doing. Suddenly, you are not the only special one.

Comparison is a slippery slope. "Comparison is the thief of joy." –Theodore Roosevelt. We all do it. Spending time looking outside of ourselves, searching for happiness. Whether you do it on your way to work, while you're at work, when you're sitting at a café people watching, or even from the comforts of your own home- scrolling through Instagram and Facebook. Comparison is always there, waiting for you to jump on board. When you begin to unravel what comparison is and where it comes from- you can bring awareness to the underlying truth. What lies beneath comparison is fear. Fear of not being enough, and the ultimate fear of not surviving.

With everything in life there is always the opportunity to give your power away. The illusion of control is always hiding behind or beneath life and as soon as we believe that we can or do have control over something- comparison and fear come swooping in. Believing that we have control creates an attachment- an energy. That energy, that was once within you, is now attached to something outside of yourself- convincing you that you won't feel a certain way unless you have it- and can hold onto it.

I'm sharing this because I believe that when it comes to anything in life- awareness of our tendencies to control and our underlying belief systems is truly the first step to living consciously. It's where freedom lies. Once you begin to do this work and practice awareness in your life, things that once had power no longer contain the same charge. They are just what they are. This relates to food, people, jobs, status, money, consumption, behavior, and thoughts. It's all related.

I still take part in comparison. Why? Because I am human. I always say, that the second you think you are 'enlightened', completely evolved or healed- you know that you are taking part in control. Part of living this life is about being human. Humans have minds and we have egos. There are times when I get caught up in old patterns: self-destruction, comparison, self-sabotage and self-hatred. Part of living in awareness is in the practice of allowing old patterns, behaviors and thoughts to come up and to allow them to just be there to sit in it. To recognize why they are there, how they came to be there, and why they are coming up. There is always the opportunity to learn more, to grow more and to become more aware.

Sometimes, I catch myself scrolling through Instagram and going through other Holistic Health Practitioners websites- and comparing. Suddenly, I am caught in the internal dialogue of "I am not good enough" once again as I look at their accounts, their works, their writing and their offerings and I feel like they have something that I don't. Suddenly, I feel like I want to be them and to feel special. This is no different to what I experienced as a child at Broadway shows. It's all the same. And it's here to humble us, and to teach us to keep moving, to embrace change and recognize the underlying unconditional element that connects us all.

Despite these consistent thoughts, behaviours and patterns- what never changes is the desire to love myself. That is always there. And I have no doubt that it's within you as well. We are all here to learn to love ourselves and embrace what is already and always here.

So it's time to drop comparison. To practice humility. And to allow yourself to fully embrace this, its time to recognize and give light to the love that has always been and will always be within you.

chloe's
COUNTERTOP

I've spent the past 5 years in this industry growing, learning and observing others in this space. I've worked in several different holistic arenas and have truly acquainted myself with two models of living and business: fear and love. What I have found is that as with any other industry in this world- competition is there and no matter what you have done or who you are- there is always someone coming behind you and being inspired by you. There is no such thing as original thought...I don't think! We are all very much creatures of evolution and of our environment and we are all being influenced and inspired by each other. It used to be that recipes were original if 70% of the recipe was unique. Now, I'm not so sure.

You would have to live in a dark cave (or under a rock) in order to prove that your recipe is totally original. And that is ok. We are here to learn from each other. It is not about who did it first, who is the best and who is best known. Instead, what I have observed over the past 5 years is the people who tend to survive and thrive- are the ones who truly practice the paradigm of community. It's not always about getting there first, being the first, or standing alone in your success.

Before beginning my business- I worked for different companies and part of my role was consulting, offering ideas and creating for them. If I were operating from a pure place of fear, then this creative process would have been stunted and destructive at the least. And sometimes, it was. When I was operating from fear, the times I offered a recipe, an idea or a contact- I felt as though I was giving something away and losing part of myself. However, what I have found- is that knowledge is here to be shared and wisdom is a gift. We are not here to be the best and to be celebrated forever. We are here to build. We are here to support. We are a community. We are all connected.

This is what my book is about. I wanted to create a space where I could share my ideas, my thoughts and my wisdom- so that others could take part in this beautiful life. I truly believe that a true life is one that is lived from a place of love. Living from fear means hiding, harboring and ultimately, holding back.

So without further adieu,

Here are my secrets to Living Consciously and Eating Intuitively.

WHO IS CHLOE?

I was born in Calgary during the Calgary Stampede of 1988. I loved being Canadian and from the moment I could speak I was never shy to proclaim my heritage, despite having two very British parents. When I just turned 5 years old, our family moved to Kuala Lumpur, Malaysia, where I called home until the end of High School. In the theme of loving Canada, every summer, upon returning from our time in Calgary, I would beg and plead and write numerous diary entries about wanting to move home to Canada. So, not surprisingly, as soon as I graduated from high school- I relocated to Vancouver, and joined my brother at the University of British Columbia where I studied Psychology and English.

My high school and university years were difficult. I battled severe eating disorders and depression throughout, and lived in the mind of a very destructive, hateful and anxious girl. I never felt like I was quite happy or comfortable and I was very lost in my world of what to do with my life. I enjoyed psychology and loved English, but I didn't know how or what to do with it. I felt very powerless and debilitated, and a lot of the time my anxiety ran the show.

When I look back on my University years (and the last few years of High School) I realize that my life was dictated by anxiety. I rarely went to class, and simple tasks like going for lunch, coffee or even grocery shopping were an issue for me. I always cared so deeply about how I looked, and I was never satisfied with my body. I spent many, many hours at the gym, and if I didn't go to the gym for at least an hour each day, that day would be ruined and lifeless. I would punish myself, starve myself, and hope for a better outcome another day.

Once I graduated from university a progressive shift began to take place. My eating disorder was less powerful than it had been and my interest in food began to grow. I started cooking more than I had in the past and began to really enjoy reading cookbooks, watching cooking shows and engulfing in the world of food. One major influence on me was my boyfriend at the time. I must say that a lot of my own realizations around a passion for food were introduced through him (thank you). He is not only a very talented chef, but he is also very passionate about sharing

chloe's
COUNTERTOP

> **"**
> *I became a Holistic Nutritionist, and my life changed in the most beautiful way, forever.*

food with others and getting people together with the focal point of food. Also, he had absolutely no fears around eating and enjoying food. So, naturally, I became his sous-chef and over the years we hosted many dinner parties. Enter major food passion. Enter community.

Suddenly, I began looking into food vocations. I looked into many culinary programs- however, the main thing that held me back from entering that world was that I had become a vegetarian several years back (partly ethical, partly eating disorder and health related) and couldn't stomach the idea of working with animal products, let alone eating and tasting them. My intuition knew it wasn't for me.

Simultaneously, I was very interested in the Dietetics program, and had been doing a lot of investigation into it. I also just so happened to be working at Whole Foods and was surrounded by a lot of fellow foodie lovers. One of which, a co-worker, who was also attending a program to become a Holistic Nutritionist. I will get into this later when I speak about Holistic Nutrition, but in keeping it short, I wasn't impressed with the designation. However, somehow, someway, a few weeks later, I found myself on the other end of a call to the administrator of the school I would soon call home. One visit later and I was enrolled to begin studying in just 2 weeks.

The rest as they say, is history. I became a Holistic Nutritionist, and my life changed in the most beautiful way, forever.

I started Chloe's Countertop just a few months before finishing the year-long program. It all happened so fast, I can barely understand or truly remember. I was coming to a point in my life where I began hearing myself and my intuitive voice much stronger than I had in a long time. I had been a writer all of my life and all throughout elementary school to high school I kept journals and diaries and wrote regularly. Looking back, I notice that when I went to University, I suddenly stopped writing and therefore, my intuitive voice was silenced.

For me, writing is a way to connect with a much deeper part of me and to release forms of anxiety that are completely consuming. So I started Chloe's Countertop. It all started one week, when I had the idea that I finally wanted to begin a blog, after years and years of thinking about it. I wanted to begin a blog where I could share all of my thoughts about nutrition and wellness and share my new recipes. I called my brother and told him that I needed to meet with him immediately. So, we met at 49th and Parallel (Vancouver) and we created Chloe's Countertop. That night, I stayed up all night, starting the Wordpress blog, designing my brand, and writing thousands of words to get things started.

I wasn't expecting much. I didn't know if people would read my writing or appreciate it at all. I don't even think I thought about it. I was doing it completely for me, with no thought or comprehension of what would come out of it or who would be involved. For the first time in a long time, I just did. I didn't think.

What happened was a complete surprise. People loved what I wrote, they associated with what I wrote and they enjoyed my recipes. It was such a big moment for me. I had that warm feeling, that it was just right. Like suddenly, I was seen. And so I continued to write, and write and write.

WHAT IS HOLISTIC NUTRITION?

THE QUESTION OF THE DECADE!

To be honest, Holistic Nutrition is a complex subject about more things than one. It is not just about your health and it is not just about whether or not you have a disease or imbalance. Holistic Nutrition is about life; it's about living. It embodies every facet of your world, and everything that is unique to you. Holistic is defined in the Webster dictionary as "relating to or concerned with complete systems rather than with individual parts". In essence, the word speaks for itself. Webster defines 'nutrition' as the act or process of nourishing or being nourished; specifically : the sum of the processes by which an animal or plant takes in and utilizes food substances. When you put it together- these two words create something around the following: the sum of all parts and systems of your life, which come together to nourish your being.

When I first heard of the designation, Holistic Nutritionist, I judged it negatively. In my head, all I could see was a bunch of hippies throwing around diagnoses

while wearing yoga pants and smoking weed. Now, this isn't to say that there are holistic nutritionist' out there who don't wear yoga pants and smoke weed. In fact, I know quite a few of them (and love them dearly). However, in my incredibly academic mind, at that time, I had judged that it was not a worthy career. I needed a degree. I needed something that I could put beside my name, feel proud about and underneath it all, I wanted to feel safe.

It's funny how things can happen (no coincidences here). It turns out; it was this world of holistic nutrition that ended up not only leaving me incredibly proud (when I'm stuck in my ego state) but also safer than ever. I discovered my calling and my true passion. I found the thing that I literally spend every hour of everyday thinking about, talking about and dreaming about. It challenges me constantly, it scares me and rewards me in everyway. It parallels what I think life is.

So, to get into the nitty gritty of what we study to become Holistic Nutritionists, I'll keep it to the brief subjects, just so you have an idea.

The courses I studied include:

- Fundamentals of Nutrition

- Biological Chemistry

- Ayurveda

- Herbal Medicine

- Pathology

- Body Metabolism

- Physiology and Anatomy

- Psychology of Disease

- Symptomatology

- Professional Skills

- Professional Practice

- Nutritional Research

- Infant and Child Nutrition

- Comparative Diets

- Natural Food/Food Preparation

> 66
>
> *We are all looking to be loved,*
> *because love is life.*

As you can tell from the diverse range of subjects, Holistic Nutrition study's every area of the human body, spirit and mind and more importantly, it focuses on each individual separately. What I mean by this is that it looks at each person as a unique entity and subject. There is no one size fits all- and therefore, there is no uniform protocol or treatment design for a group of people. Instead, it takes into

consideration both sides of the debate- nature AND nurture. We are influenced by our surroundings, where we come from, who our family is, where and how we were educated, what we've eaten, what we haven't eaten, what our home life was like, what we've been exposed to...and the list goes on.

So when you take this all into consideration you can understand why my entire paradigm about this subject flipped when I began studying it. Suddenly, I realized that these "hippies" were not only very intelligent and in-tune with the world, they were sensitive, hard-working and conscious beings. It takes a certain type of person (or a certain time of your life) to dedicate yourself to a healing practice. As with many careers and life choices, it is so humbling when you begin to work in service of something much bigger than you. It isn't always easy...sometimes it's even heartbreaking.

For me one of the things I have loved most about Holistic Nutrition is that it has allowed me to be who I am and evolve as naturally as possible. It introduced me to a world that I had previously judged out of fear and discomfort. A space that I now call home. It makes me so happy to witness the world globally and gradually

embrace holistic health, as each day, more and more people appreciate the gifts that healing can offer.

One of the fundamental facets of this world is that it is about true healing and presence. Throughout my education, there were so many moments of crazy confusion and frustration. Going from one end of the nutrition spectrum one week (raw and vegan) to a complete opposite the next (Paleolithic and bone broth)- it was such a reflection of life itself. We are not all the same (on the surface) and so many of us live our lives focusing too much in these extremes.

To me, the beauty of life comes from the oxymoron that we are all different and yet we are all one. No matter where you go in this world, you will experience similar interactions, emotions and relationships with incredibly different people. We all look different, speak different languages and have different beliefs- but what unites us is the simple fact that we are all running off of two very contrasting innate states: fear and love.

We are all looking to be loved, because love is life.

In holistic nutrition there is no right way to be and there is no wrong way to live. There tends to be a stigma that holistic nutrition equals a raw and vegan lifestyle. That's actually not true. During my studies, I was surrounded by a lot of HCLF (high carb low fat) people; however, there were also meat

eaters, people of all weights and sizes and from different ethnic backgrounds. Not everyone ate fully raw and not everyone ate 100% organic.

I was introduced to a concept through a good friend of mine, which made so much sense to me. Also, I actually have this conversation with my partner quite frequently. The concept is the idea that we are all evolving individuals and we are all at different levels of evolution. If you believe in spirits and reincarnation, then you will know that some people come back to this world to re-learn a lesson or to teach. You know the sayings "old soul" and "kindred spirit"?

To me, these phrases speak to the idea that some of us are more spiritually evolved than others. The most important thing to note when you begin to get into this way of thinking and this space of living, is that as soon as you go into judgment you have checked out of consciousness. There is no right or wrong way to live, and neither one of us is better than the other.

I think that this is such an important concept right now in this world. We are at a place where many of us are embracing the idea of spirituality and consciousness, and living a more conscious life. The thing about human beings is that we are always on a spiritual sea-saw, balancing between being truly present and living from intuition, and being caught up in our egos. Judgment is a behavior of the ego; it is a representation of power and separation. As soon as you begin to go into judgment you are removing yourself from another, and believing that you are different. The truth is that there is no separation and we are all connected; we are all one.

I have noticed this topic come up more and more, and it's sometimes challenging because my own ego wants to control it, and think that I am more evolved and therefore better able to "fix" it.

I truly dedicate where I am to my life-altering choice to study Holistic Nutrition and begin Chloe's Countertop, it has taught me so much. It has brought me endless amounts of joy and un-ending lessons in humility. It constantly catches me in an ego trip.

To end this portion of the book, I have 11 lessons that my Holistic Nutrition journey has taught me:

1. Judgment is a behavior of the ego, we are not separate from one another

2. When you are on an ego-trip, take a breath and speak honestly from the heart

3. When anger surfaces, take a moment to notice what you are resisting

4. Discomfort and pain are helpful experiences, embrace them

5. Sometimes, our largest pain points are our greatest gifts

6. Each body is different, works differently, likes different things and has different levels of optimization (aka we are not all supposed to look the same)

7. When you are feeling ill feelings towards someone, take a moment to send them love and understand where these emotions are coming from- it is usually not about the surface reason

8. The way we feel about others is usually a reflection of how we feel about ourselves

9. We are most drawn to qualities in others that we love about ourselves and don't recognize

10. Food is energy and its energy is impacted from the moment it is created (production, harvesting, packaging, consumption)

11. The way you feel about the food that you are eating directly influences how your body processes it

> 66
>
> *as soon as you go into judgment you have checked out of consciousness. There is no right or wrong way to live, and neither one of us is better than the other.*

chloe's
COUNTERTOP

A HOLISTIC NUTRITIONIST'S 10 NON-NEGOTIABLES IN LIFE

When you begin to look at yourself as a complete unit; a system, you can start to approach your life in a way that complements every part of you and considers your mind, body and soul as opposed to just one or even none at all. When I started studying to become a Holistic Nutritionist, my whole world was literally blown away because I began to realize how much of me I was neglecting in the way I approached my life. I was eating for weight only, I was exercising for weight and appearance only, and I was in relationships to satisfy my mind and parts of my heart, as opposed to my whole.

With modern western medicine, when we get sick, we tend to manage illness with one area of life: medicine/pharmaceuticals. We don't think of the emotional and spiritual source or foundation of illness. We know that it's important to sleep, but that's about it.

What I have come to learn is that the way to approach anything in life starts from the source: you. This is where self-love and self-care is so important. If you don't take care of you, there is no way you can do what you are here to do or truly help

anyone else. This is one big lesson I learnt during the first few months of my career as a Holistic Nutritionist. When I graduated, suddenly, I felt like I had all the tools in my kit to help anyone and everyone around me. I wanted to heal everyone. What I soon realized is that this method is not only unsustainable, it basically wears you down and you stop getting dinner invitations very quickly. No one likes a preacher. A preacher is separate, better than and removed from. Mahatma Gandhi said it perfectly, "you must be the change you wish to see in the world." And so it is true.

This is where it all begins. Holistic Nutrition is about caring for yourself and directing as much energy inwards as you are outwards. It is about balance.

The beauty of this is that you do not need to be a Holistic Nutritionist to practice and know these 10 Non-Negotiables. These are universal lessons that we should all know and practice.

1. NATURAL RESOURCES

It is no secret that Holistic Nutritionist' rely on Mother Nature big time. Our tool kits are filled with her gifts (essential oils, natural products, food, water and herbal medicinals) and nature is where we first turn when in need of a boost, some therapy or support. When you begin to look at everything in the world that humans use and rely on- you realize that it all stems from Mother Nature: shelter, security, medicine and consumption. What differentiates normal consumption to holistic consumption is the concept of consciousness. Conscious consumption is the idea of not only knowing where things come from, but also how they were produced, how they effect the environment and how you can give back. Without sustainability, there are no natural resources. So ask yourself, where does this product come from and what is it made of?

2. SLEEP AND NOURISHMENT

Aka self care. You will have a challenging time finding a Holistic Nutritionist who does not value sleep and good food. In fact, these are usually at the top of their list. These are the fundamentals. Without sleep, our bodies cannot function properly and support us in what we need to do. It is during sleep that many essential functions take place, including one of the most important physiological stages of relaxation and repair. When we are awake, we tend to be switched on and functioning in over-drive (stress), so sleep is not only helpful it is completely fundamental.

Nourishment relates to not only what you eat but also everything you put in and on your body. Fun fact: your skin is your largest organ! What you put on it matters. When you begin to think of your body as an actual living being (which it is) you realize that it is a machine that has needs in order to be efficient. Just like your car needs gas, and your nice car needs specific gas- our bodies rely on specific nutrients in order to stay moving.

Toxins are a big "no-no" in a Holistic Nutritionist's book and when you begin to investigate what are in some of the products out there, where they come from and what they do to us, they will no doubt be removed from your life as well! My advice: check your labels, read up on common household toxins and begin empowering yourself in this area.

3. COMMUNITY AND A TRIBE

This is a big one. We are social beings. We require love and support (not only from within but externally too). Another common theme of Holistic Nutritionists is the good old "friend-cleanse" that takes place during or after school. The idea is that throughout your life you tend to collect people and depending on who you are and your fixation- you can be a bit of a hoarder of friends and people to fill space. When you begin to practice self-love and self-care, you not only realize that you don't need as much as you thought- but you also begin to realize what relationships in your life are toxic or not-supportive of who you truly are.

Our communities are so important and whom we spend our time with directly affects what we do and how we do it. Is your family and friends supportive of who you truly are and do you feel comfortable being completely you with them? These are questions to begin thinking about when you start living in balance- and embracing a true life of happiness. The fundamental idea is to surround yourself with unconditional love and support. The rest is just unnecessary and energy-draining noise.

4. MORNINGS

If you are on social media and follow websites like Well & Good, Huffington Post, Elephant Journal and Mind Body Green- you will know by now that mornings are important to us holistic kids. We love our mornings. When you sit back and think about it, it makes sense- mornings are what set your day. When we have a "bad morning", chances are, we get stuck in this zone and our entire day thereafter is affected. Am I right?

If we wake up in the morning and immediately get stuck in doing things for others- we are setting the tone that we are here for others and will always compromise ourselves. As natural healers, it is important for us to make the time and intention on putting focus to our own needs and support.

Usually, this means a moment of meditation in the morning, movement, nourishment and rest.

> *Nourishment relates not only to what you eat but also to what you put in and on your body – physically, emotionally and spiritually.*

5. MOVEMENT

Movement is a vital part of life. We need movement in order to flush toxins, pump blood and to breath. There are systems in our body that require movement in order to function properly and our bodies are naturally designed to move. If we weren't supposed to move we would not have legs, arms and a cardiovascular system that is designed to support cardiovascular activity. We are meant to move. This doesn't mean that you must go into a gym and spend an hour on a treadmill or elliptical, playing a tape of "I'm not good enough" while just barely breaking a sweat. If a treadmill or elliptical is what helps you to feel good- then go for it. However, the idea is that movement is a natural function and it naturally releases endorphins, which naturally make us feel good. When you begin to think of everything in the way that Mother Nature designed it to be- you can not only appreciate it more but you can begin to take part in it without the typical judgment, attachment and heaviness of the human ego. In other words, get moving and do what makes you happy and helps you to feel good. Also, turn the "I'm not good enough" tape off, or better yet- throw it out!

6. AN UNDERSTANDING OF YOUR GREATER PURPOSE/HUMILITY

When you begin to do something purely because you love it, something magical happens. You realize that there is something much greater than yourself that is taking space. The major downfall with doing things for money and success is that you can get incredibly stuck in this limited space of living where your purpose

is money and/or success. We all know the quote, "money can't buy happiness". I believe that this is the reason why.

Happiness is not a fabrication of the human condition- it is a pure emotion that can be evoked from the simplest of experiences. Happiness is everywhere and it can be found in the strangest and most un-assuming places. For instance, whenever I travel to India or somewhere like it (where the general global view is that it is a place of poverty and unhappiness) I am so humbled by how happy people are, regardless of how much money they have or how "successful" they are. The simplest way to get outside of this limited paradigm of living is to do something for another. The act of giving is one of the most magical ways to experience life and when you remove your 'self' from the equation, your worldview expands significantly and you can begin to live from a place much larger than just 'me, myself and I'.

7.   PASSION

Passion is big. I find passion a difficult concept in a lot of ways because we tend to define passion as something that is outside of what we do everyday. The traditional careers and roles of the Western

chloe's
COUNTERTOP

world do not leave much space for passion (doctor, lawyer, police officer, pilot) and as a result, I think they have given passion a bad name. When we think of passion we think of the 'starving artist' who has chosen to live a life without success and money and is thus, starving?

When I chose to become a Holistic Nutritionist what I found was the complete opposite. Once you discover what passion is, you realize that passion doesn't fit in a box and it isn't limited to what we categorize as a hobby. Passion is everywhere. Passion is a perspective. We are not here to live a passion-less life. The first step is in finding what makes you feel good and what you love. It doesn't have to be complicated and it doesn't have to be one thing. You can be passionate about many things; heck- you can be passionate about everything, if you please. Just start somewhere- find something that makes you happy and begin injecting it into your daily practice. You may find that you not only live happier but that passion is showing up in many areas of your life, waiting for you to see it.

8. ROUTINE

Ah, routine. How I love you.

For a while, I started neglecting routine because I began associating it with what we refer to as a 'control-freak'. Basically, routine was for the Monica's ('Friends' reference) of the world. Now, this may be true- but I also think that routine can mean many different things. It doesn't have to mean an exercise routine, or an eating routine.

Routine can mean, waking up in the morning and brushing your teeth. Human bodies are big fans of routines- it is what helps them function properly. We all run

off of a 'biological clock', which maintains overall function and rhythm in the body. Our bodies love knowing when to wake up, when to go to sleep, when to eat, when to digest, when to remove waste, etc. It is all part of the efficient machine we live in. The idea is to embrace routine, support it and notice when we are out of it. When we fall out of a routine we can get emotionally affected. Here's the key: just notice it and slowly bring yourself back into what makes you and your body feel good. Every body is different, get to know yours and understand what it likes.

9.   AWARENESS

What many of these points have in common is the concept of awareness. Awareness is such a crucial part of a holistic life- and it really just means bringing attention to something. It doesn't mean judging it, changing it, fixing it or feeling bad about it. It doesn't involve attaching to it either. It just means, noticing it.

Falling out of your routine? Notice it. Feeling sad? Notice it. Feeling happy? Notice it. Begin to bring attention to the ebbs and flows of your life and notice how each experience affects how you feel and what you do. Each person tends to be a little different and whether you attach to things, run away from things, or move towards things- just notice what your tendency is... so that you can begin to understand who you truly are.

10. BOUNDARIES

Last but most certainly not least, boundaries. As healers this is probably one of the most important non-negotiable to learn. We all need boundaries and maintaining and communicating our boundaries is not a bad thing and it doesn't make us a bad person. Actually, it's the opposite. If you live without any boundaries, you can end up running yourself to the ground, depending on how sensitive of a person you are.

I am an incredibly sensitive person, and an empath, so for me- setting boundaries has been an amazingly important lesson. Without my boundaries, I was taking on every single person's energy, problems and emotions and I was left completely drained, compromising and neglecting my self.

This entire category relates to self-care, and the idea of taking care of you before taking care of another. Without boundaries you cannot be balanced at work, in relationships, with friends and with family. In fact, family is almost always one of the most important areas to have boundaries in. So notice where you are giving too much of yourself and where you feel like you are being 'taken advantage of'. Begin to visualize putting a boundary up to not only protect yourself but to also communicate where you need some space.

So there you have it- the 10 non-negotiables of a Holistic Nutritionist. Well, really it's the 10 non-negotiables of a happy and and balanced person. As they say, "there's no better time than the present". So, why not get started with your happy life and choose one of these areas to bring your attention to today. You'd be surprised by how similar we all really are.

chloe's
COUNTERTOP

LIVING IN TRUTH

All my life I've been taught about truth. My mum ingrained it"s importance in my brother and I. We deeply feared the consequences of not telling the truth. She would always say, "nothing is more important than the truth". Looking back, I realize this to be true and feel the authenticity and depth of knowing in the quote "the truth will set you free". How incredible is it, that all we have to do in order to be free, is to tell the truth?

So why don't we do it? Why do we hide so cowardly and spinelessly in the darkness, in our stories and in our denial? Even the people who claim to be truth-seekers and truth-holders are running away. We live in a society that is deeply rooted in fear. Our decisions are motivated by fear, our choices are underlined by desire and we are constantly living off of the robotic ways: pleasure seeking or pain avoiding.

So what is truth and how do you live it? When I was younger I didn't completely understand what truth represented. For me, little white lies held no damage and caused no destruction. They were just what they were, little white lies. Necessary.

I'll never forget the moment, in high school, when I came face to face with truth's power. This was all during a time when my health, wellness, sanity and balance were compromised by a modern-day disease too many girls (and boys) fall victim to. Eating disorders, bulimia, anorexia, depression and suicidal tendencies. I was caught in this web of imbalance and all of my choices, decisions and desires were led by fear, running away and avoiding pain. I did whatever I felt like doing when I felt like doing it. I was so cut off from my intuition and a deep sense of knowing, which I now believe we are all born with and unfortunately move away from as we age.

I would spend my days telling myself horrible things, pressuring myself to be and look a certain way and I was drawn to things that were in no way good for me. I was caught in a conflict- of feeling and wanting love and being taken over so intensely by fear and darkness. The best way to illustrate this battle was my ferocious need for love and to feel loved. I would do anything to feel wanted by another person.

It felt obsessive and without it I felt like I couldn't breath. Boyfriends and boys in general were the most important thing to me- and they were all I could really think about. I just wanted everyone to like me and to want me.

I attended an American International School system in a Muslim country. In other words, drugs were strongly prohibited. We were drug tested on the regular at random, and it was just a known fact to stay away from drugs and marijuana. Even though our neighboring British International School friends were known for their weed smoking behaviours, most of us knew it just wasn't worth it. We had heard many horror stories of families being deported, parents losing their jobs and school records being tainted- all for one plant-induced high.

> ##
> ## *we are constantly living off the robotic ways: pleasure seeking or pain avoiding*

And then my friend from Australia came for a visit. We were smoking buddies (the non-marijuana kind) and it felt good to have her back. One night we were out with our British School friends and she grabbed herself a 'doobie' to bring home with us. And here I was, faced with the same battle I dealt with on a daily basis. Do I follow this rebellion on a path to be liked and accepted or do I listen to the voice inside of me that is yelling "Noooooo!"

I rolled into school that Monday morning feeling intensely uneasy about my choices and the imminent consequences my Mum always spoke about. What if they find out? How much is too much? My mind was running in circles and my heart wouldn't stop racing. As I sat in my first class that morning (Theory of Knowledge) I had a sense that something bad was coming. I was screwed. In she walked, the principle's secretary with the white piece of paper. On it, was the name of a student who would make their way to the nurses' office to have strands of hair cut from their head to be sent for drug testing. Despite the fact that it was impossible for me to see whose name was on that paper or know in any way- I knew it was me. I felt it. Sweat stains graced the fabric of my school blue shirt. As she passed the paper to my hunky Australian teacher, I prepared myself for the execution I was about to face.

"Chloe Elgar" he proclaimed in a confident and annoyingly sexy Aussie voice.

I tried my best to brush it off and look as calm as possible as everyone looked towards me and threw fist punches and high-fives my way. My mission to be cool and popular was a successful one in school and I suppose I made it look like nothing was going to phase me. I picked myself up, accepted the heavy, soul-crushing white paper from his hands and walked out of the classroom. As the door closed, panic and anxiety took over my body in more ways than one. I knew I had to walk to the nurse's office, but my body had another idea. Run. Run as fast as you can out of here. In a matter of fight or flight, flight encompassed my being as the crimson blood rushed to my limbs encouraging me to speed out of school. Instead, I ran to the theatre garden and pulled my phone out of my pocket.

"Yes? Is everything ok?"

I couldn't speak. I could barely breath.

"Chloe? What's wrong? Where are you? Come to my office, I just go to school."

A warm sense leaked into my body as I ran to my Mum's classroom. I told her everything. I told her what I did. I told what was about to happen. I couldn't imagine a way out. I started speaking about dying, and leaving and how I felt like "it was over". I wanted to rip my skin off. How could I be so stupid? She sat and listened, gathered her thoughts and said:

"Chloe, you have to tell the truth."

That day after fighting my Mum for a few minutes, I turned around, walked out of her classroom and stepped right into the Principle's office. In a panic, I told him that I needed to speak to him and tell him something, despite feeling like this choice could be the end of me. What if I was kicked out of school? What if he told everyone? What if my life was over? What if he hated me? What if, what if, what if.

After telling him my story and filling him in on what was going on in my life- I went to the nurse's office and took the drug test. I was put on a "light-sentenced" probation (meaning I had to take the week off of school) and my sports' coaches were informed of my decision. Some of it truly sucked. Some of it I wish never happened. However, the truth is, I am so happy that I decided to go with telling the truth. Despite the setbacks and the disappointments I created, there is no comparison to the way I felt when I sat in the principle's office and allowed myself to be me; mistakes and all.

Looking back, I realize that this life-changing choice wasn't the last example of a time I battled with telling the truth and fibbing to get away with a rebellious choice. I still made mistakes and I still dealt with many, many consequences thereafter.

Since then, telling the truth has become a bit of a mission for me. Chloe's Countertop is all about the truth. It was created from a deep desire to begin to

66

Part of living in light is living in truth. I always say that the most important person to be honest with is you.

share my life; to write about my stories, my thoughts and experiences. To release energies that had been trapped in my being for too long.

It turns out, telling the truth is one of the greatest gifts that we have. And the positive reinforcement is undeniable. What if we brought our children up influencing and inspiring them to be authentic through our own actions? What if we chose to share a little more about our lives? Why do we choose to live in the dark? Why do we choose to harbor our thoughts and attack ourselves for wanting to release them? After all, they are just thoughts. They are not who we are, they are just a part of us. Our thoughts do not define us and our experiences are not our essence.

Part of living in light is living in truth. I always say that the most important person to be honest with is you. Start at the root. Start with the foundation. Ask yourself these questions and answer them with a curiosity to go deeper.

- How are you feeling?

- What are your thoughts?

- What are you hiding from?

- What are you most scared of?

- Is there something you aren't doing because of fear?

- Are you ashamed of something in your past?

- Do you feel stuck somewhere?

- Do you feel alive? If not, why?

- Are you happy? If not, why?

- Do you want to be happy? If not, why?

- Do you love you? Do you feel love?

- What's stopping you?

- Where/what/who are you feeling drawn to?

There is a lot of ways to begin to tell the truth. Sometimes, it's easiest to start with you. There are a lot of ways that we can rationalize and justify why the truth shouldn't be told or why it isn't necessary- however, the truth is, the truth will always set you free and you must always begin with the truth.

WHAT IS INTUITIVE EATING?

This phrase seems to be circulating a lot lately and when you really take it apart to understand what it means- it's pretty simple. It all relates to cravings and messages from your body. As a result of the diet industry, we have been taught and conditioned to cut the connection between our minds and our bodies. We no longer know how to respond to the signs and signals that our bodies send us- to tell us something. When we are sick, we respond with pharmaceuticals, which shut off the connection even further. When we are tired, we drink caffeine or take other substances to ignore that message. When we are injured, we take certain substances to shut off the signal to our brain, and we no longer feel the pain. In every space of life, we have created ways to disconnect our minds from our bodies.

When you take a look at the diet industry- every single message out there is about learning to have "willpower", to be in control and to be disciplined. We are taught to respond to our bodies cravings by either ignoring them, taking something to make it go away, or to choose something else that will superficially satisfy that craving.

What ends up happening, is that over time this method is not sustainable. We have been conditioned to believe that cravings are a bad thing and a sign of weakness.

We are all emotional eaters

It all starts when someone mentions that they want eating to not be emotional, or that they want to approach their health from a completely non-emotional place. My answer: it's impossible.

66

Eating is emotional. We are all emotional eaters.

Eating is emotional. We are all emotional eaters. Think about it, each of us eat three times a day, every single day of our lives (if we're fortunate to have the gift of food). That is 1,095 times a year. For a 27 year old, like myself, that's 29,565 times in my current lifetime. That is a lot of eating. It's a lot of anything. The repetition of this behavior is something that creates a pattern within you. An innate behavior, if you will. This is not just a behavior that you enjoy doing, it is also something that you must do in order to survive.

Humans can survive without food for 3 weeks. Without food, we wouldn't be alive (this is excluding the miraculous examples of sadhus and other spiritual and religious devout who go without food for extended periods of time). So we need food to survive.

Looking into the biology of eating and the neuroscience, it quickly becomes clear that food is emotional. The act of eating is stimulated by the more than just your physical body. The act of eating does more than just stimulate your tummy. Eating can stimulate emotional memories. Eating can stimulate happiness.

When you begin to dive into the rabbit hole of understanding hunger, eating and emotions, you begin to understanding that the entire of act of eating is quite complex. It is never just about one aspect of us. We are physical, mental, emotional and spiritual beings. Have you noticed that your hunger can vary, depending on what you are doing and how you are feeling? So many variables can affect your hunger: travel, energy, sleep (or lack thereof), anxiety, movement, stress, emotion.

Intuitive eating is a journey.

Conscious living is a journey.

You can start here, with these steps:

1. Get rid of the scale, it's not about a number

2. Be conscious of how you speak to yourself

3. Treat your body with the same respect and love it offers you

4. Put your attention towards your internal language: what do you say to yourself when you are stressed, anxious or uncomfortable?

5. What are your beliefs? Where do they come from?

6. Why are you hungry? What are you hungry for?

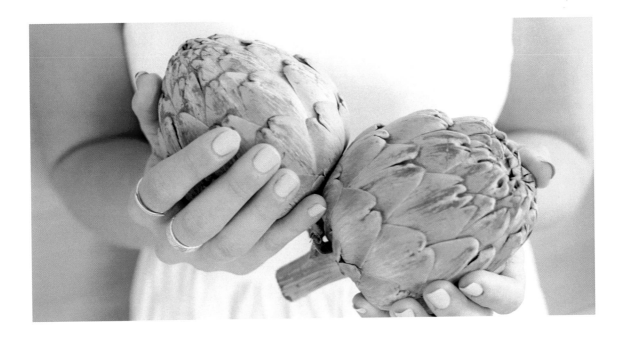

So what are cravings? In nutrition, we learn that cravings are signs that our bodies are deficient in something- a macro nutrient or a micronutrient. In order to strengthen and reawaken that connection- you have to start listening and responding to your body more consistently. If you feel tired, rest. If you are experiencing pain, look into where the pain is coming from and why so you can address it appropriately. If you have a craving for a certain food, ask yourself what you are hungry for and then eat that food. Sure, choose the best quality of it, but also- sometimes you just have to eat it. We have created such a complex game of out eating- that we have truly lost sight of what eating is really about.

Eating is nourishment.

Eating is energy. It's our fuel.

This is what intuitive eating is about. It is about re-strengthening and awakening the connection between your mind and your body.

Next time you are craving something, eat it.

Don't think about it. Don't decide whether or not it is good for you, how many calories it is, how it will effect your body or how much you will need to run to burn it off. Just eat it.

WHAT IS CONSCIOUS EATING?

I love it when the world just clicks. When everything starts to make sense and all of a sudden, you are right where you are meant to be. For me, that is what conscious eating and intuitive living is about. After many, many years of working and living in this space- I feel as though I have stumbled upon the holistic living gold mine.

MEDITATION:

To start, I want you to take a moment to breath.

Plant your feet on the ground or sit cross-legged and lengthen your spine towards the sky.

Close your eyes, and visualize light. Sitting in a pure state of consciousness, breathe through your nose and count to 4.

Imagine filling your belly with this air, feeling it travel from the tip of your nose to the base of your toes, engulfing every cell with oxygen.

As you breath out for 4 counts, feel each molecule of carbon dioxide leave your body, leaving each cell nourished with hydrogen.

Do this 4 times, or until you feel calm and light.

Now, I want you to say the word 'conscious eating', and feel the word as you spell it out into your soul space. Feel each syllable and each letter.

ASK YOURSELF:

What does this word feel like?

What comes up for you when you say this word?

What does it represent?

For me, conscious eating is all about putting thought, feeling and awareness to the act of eating. It is about being mindful. Before I started doing this work, I was heavily engulfed in bulimia. All of my eating behaviours were completely void of consciousness and I was running off of something else. There was something, deep beyond the act of eating, that was driving my hunger and my consumption. Instead of thinking about what I was going to eat, and eating it with every cell in my body- I would have an immediate moment of panic for some reason, followed by a very fast episode of consumption. During this time I would eat every single thing that I could think of and could get my hands on. This, of course, was followed by a forced episode of purging the food from my body, and the after-effects of nausea, exhaustion, blood sugar instability and emotional distress.

So when I talk about conscious eating it is quite opposite to my old patterns of bulimia.

To start eating consciously, begin with a few of these practices:

- Sitting down to eat

- Blessing your food and practicing gratitude for the simple things in your life like food, water and shelter.

- Asking yourself "am I hungry" or "am I thirsty" followed by "what am I hungry for?"

- Bringing attention to cravings to deepen your body-mind connection. What do you crave and when do you crave it?

- Chewing properly to satiate and support your body's natural stages of digestion. Chew slowly and pay attention to the way your mouth breaks down food.

- Eating intuitive portions aka not restricting yourself or trying to control your hunger

Conscious eating doesn't mean eating less or eating more, necessarily. The moment that you get excited about skipping a meal or not feeling hunger- it may be time to get uncomfortable and eat. Our minds are powerful and they are very good at tricking us- bringing us back into our coping mechanisms and strategies. What it comes down to is this: the only person that is important to be honest with, is you. Notice your tendencies to control and ask yourself in those moments: "what am I hiding from?"

Recently, I spent a transformative week co-hosting a retreat in Costa Rica where 15 women gathered to adventure, heal and fall in love with themselves and the world around them. This retreat included Ayurvedic principles around eating beahviours and all organic, local and mindfully prepared foods. In Ayurveda, the idea is that our body reaches it's highest potential in the early afternoon (around 2pm), when the sun is at it's highest point. As a result, our bodies burn the most energy at this time and require the most food. With this reasoning, our bodies are at their lowest burning potential in the evening, when the sun is down and we are preparing for rest. So with this in mind, we were eating a decently sized breakfast, a large lunch with a vegan dessert, followed by a smaller dinner (or no dinner at all). Although I absolutely agree with these principles and Ayurveda in general- I noticed some of the women's excitement when they found out about missing dinner. It takes one to know one. I immediately could tell that some women were happy to know that there

was an ancient nutritional theory to support them skipping meals, and therefore the potential of losing weight. Hello control!

The reason I am telling this story is because of the connection between what our minds' know and what our bodies' know. Our minds are incredibly powerful and useful tools- and as we know, they have done wonders for human society. In the same light, our minds have also caused a lot of pain and darkness, and I believe it comes from choosing to donate our power to our minds, and in turn, completely ignoring our bodies and our souls (intuition). When this happens, although we think (aka the mind) we are in control- we actually become enslaved to our masterminds, which is an unsustainable relationship to live in forever. If we are living from the source of our minds completely- then we are shutting off the connection to our bodies and our souls and as a result, we are not living consciously.

ALL ABOUT CHEWING

So here's the thing about chewing. It is essential. In order for your body to properly digest food (aka pass it through your system), absorb nutrients (aka stay strong and healthy) and for you to feel full and satiated (aka so you don't keep snacking)- you have to chew. In biology, chewing is also known as 'mastication'- which is the function that your mouth preforms in order to begin the stages of digestion. We all assume that everything is very mechanical and we can control our bodies/hunger/cravings with our mind. I'm here to tell you that it runs deeper than that. Again, our thoughts are powerful and they don't only impact the energy within us, how we feel and how our bodies feel- but they also affect the actual mechanical behaviors and balance.

For instance, as soon as you begin to think about food- your mouth waters, right? The act of "mouthwatering' is way more intricate than just your mouth filling with saliva when you think of food. The whole phrase comes from the concept that the thought of food stimulates digestion. Saliva is secreted from your salivary glands, which releases the enzymes (salivary enzymes) that are responsible for the primary stages of digestion, carbohydrates/sugars. This doesn't mean that it's all done for you and you can just inhale your food without breathing, thinking and chewing. When you turn to nature, as your guide for life you begin to realize that everything is here for a reason. Creation is not random. We have lungs to breath. We have teeth and mouths to chew and eat. When you were born and as an infant, chewing isn't something you were taught. It's innate. It's a natural behavior that is here for a reason. When you begin to look at life, and your body in this way, it can change not only the way that you do things and approach life, but it also allows space (massive space) for gratitude.

Be mindful.
Chew your food.

I always remember the first time I put awareness to my breath. I was in a nutrition class and we were talking about the difference between learned behaviours and innate behaviours. Basically, a learned behvaiour is something that you've been taught either directly or indirectly from your environment (nurture) where as an innate behavior is something you are born with (nature). From the moment we are born we know how to breathe, much like how a baby horse knows how to stand on it's four feet (hooves) when it is born (survival instinct). Something beyond the conscious mind directs this behavior.

The same goes for food and eating. Human babies immediately know where to get milk from and their bodies know how to digest. You don't have to think about how your body will process proteins and digest fats. The thing is, as we get older, our

innate beahviours seem to get crowded by our learned behaviours and distractions. For instance, although adults do breath (or they would die), so much of the time they aren't breathing properly. So much of yoga, exercise and meditation are about the breath and mindful-breathing. As a society, we are shallow breathers. The oxygen is not making its way through the body, to each cell, with each breath. As more and more things/thoughts come into our conscious mind- and create belief systems in our subconscious minds- our innate behaviours become limited. We breath shallow, we don't sleep enough, we are dehydrated and we crave chemicals and sweeteners that are not real food for our bodies to recognize.

When you begin to look at your body as this living being that is here to support you, it becomes a lot easier and more natural to be mindful of what it needs to live a balanced and happy life. Just think about it: every time you eat a food, your body does it's best to chew it, break it down, digest it, process and absorb it and eliminate it. Overtime, if you continue to not chew or not chew efficiently, eat food that your body doesn't recognize as food and wash it all down with stimulants and

substances that could be toxic to your body- the burden builds.

I always like to look at this through the metaphor of a bucket. Imagine that a bucket represents your body with a very small hole at the bottom. Each time something is put into your body, it goes into this bucket. Gradually and naturally, the items are processed and slowly move through the small hole. Adding water into this bucket makes the elimination process much easier and more natural. Without water, the solids items and foods just stay solid, and are not able to pass through the small hole. The other thing to keep in mind is that your body cannot differentiate between what is real and what isn't real or toxic. It all goes into the bucket. And overtime, the more refined, processed, synthetic and toxic materials added to the bucket- the less efficient it is at eliminating and going through the stages of processing.

Soon, this movement becomes stagnant and your body begins absorbing materials that are not actually good for it and are toxic. Over time, these items build and build until they over-flow, pouring out of the top of the bucket. This is a symbol of symptoms of imbalance in your body. This is when symptoms such as: acne, rashes, spots, headaches, gastrointestinal pain and in more serious cases, disease begin to show up. These are not things to hide from with medicine. These are the messages that your body is sending you to tell you that it needs some support. It needs a break, so that it can begin to clear out this toxic-build up that has taken place overtime.

So part of returning to balance involves supporting your body's innate beahviours- and going back to the basics. This relates to the chapter on holistic nutrition. And it totally connects to food and conscious eating.

Ask yourself: am I hungry? What am I craving? What am I hungry for? Am I thirsty? Am I satiated?

Be mindful.

Chew your food.

Pay attention to your bodies messages, signs and symptoms.

Support proper digestion.

CHLOE'S LIFE PLAN

If you are a part of the Chloe's Countertop Community (online) then you have already had a taste of the Chloe's Life Plan. For those of you that are completely new to this: welcome! Chloe's Life Plan is a balanced guide of living a conscious and intuitive existence. It is truly a blueprint to follow and refer to when you are feeling out of balance and in need of some love and inspiration. The idea behind it is to offer you simple tools that are easy to follow so that when things get challenging and you are out of flow- you can choose an area to focus on, to bring you back to a place of comfort and stability.

So what is flow?

In psychology, (according to Wikipedia) flow is defined as "the mental state of operation in which a person performing an activity is fully immersed in a feeling of energized focus, full involvement, and enjoyment in the process of the activity". As with everything in my life, I love to bridge the gap between varying paradigms and ways of being of understanding the world and the people in it. So, I truly feel that flow reaches beyond a mere mental state, in fact- your entire being can achieve a state of flow and it comes from being in harmony with each of your levels of being (mind, body and soul). The thing with flow is that it isn't something to be in 100% of the time for the rest of your life. We need to experience variation in order to survive and to grow and as we know, life is always changing. So the important thing to realize right now is that the challenges, discomforts, pains and problems are all an important part of life. Ebb and flow is crucial to evolution.

When I work with clients, this is one of the most important points to establish before we begin any work. We are so conditioned to believe and strive for perfection and happiness, that we truly fear and run away from pain. We attach to the good and we run away from the bad. Anything that doesn't make us feel good or doesn't make sense in our minds is pushed away, looked at as bad and not good for us- and ultimately creates more pain in our lives.

The practice here is the idea of attachment. We love to control. We love to feel like we are the reason something happened and that we have the ultimate say and choice in what happens in our lives. The great part about this is when things go "right"- we feel wonderful. The downside is that when things don't go so well we feel absolutely horrible and we tend to punish ourselves.

When I think of flow- I think of a neutral state- when you are not riding high up the roller-coaster ladder, and you are also not spiraling down. It is this state of "balance" that brings an underlying moment of non-attachment.

This is where Chloe's Life Plan comes in handy. When you have a blueprint that you create, which offers you tools to bring in awareness when you are experiencing a "high" or a "low", you will eventually create a new belief system and way of management that allow you to let go of control. In other words, when something goes wrong you don't try to fix it or stop living- you continue to live and focus your attention in re-harmonizing your states of being by putting attention elsewhere.

1. **Food:** cooking, gardening, eating, harvesting, farms
2. **Eastern Influence:** ayurveda, herbal medicine, yoga, massage, acupuncture, osteopathy
3. **Sensory Therapy:** colour, chakras, essential oils, aura soma, music/singing
4. **Animals and Nature:** horses, dogs, mountains, trees, elephants, owls, whales
5. **Water:** natural water sources (waterfalls, rivers, lakes), body 70% water
6. **Breathing/Air:** meditation, breathing, circulation
7. **Home & Community:** farmers market, family, dancing, home, space
8. **Travel/Movement:** world exploration, flying, hiking, walking, history/culture, movement
9. **Joy:** coffee, green juice, chocolate, materialism, creation, vision, pleasure
10. **Love:** sex, kissing, touch, romance, friendships, family

CREATE YOUR VISION:

It's time to get interactive. Grab your favourite journal and pen, and go within (use the meditation again if you like) to explore what these prompts bring up for you. It's time to get playful and rediscover what lies beneath.

- I want to be an...

- I'm going to make it happen by...

- I want to live in...

- I want to create...

- I want to explore...

- I want to know about...

- I want to feel...

- I love spending my mornings...

- I love listening to...

- I always admire people who...

- In 5 years, I want to be...

- to live a life of passion means...

- my 3 world truths are...

Repeat after me:

"I know that it won't be easy and there will be many challenges, but it is about the journey and I am very excited for it."

chloe's
COUNTERTOP

*it's important to put
focus into your home and
to nourish it*

CHLOE'S LIFE PLAN IS DIVIDED INTO 10 SPACES:

1. FOOD/NOURISHMENT

As you can imagine, this space relates to the things that you put into your body. For too long, we have purely looked at food as either enjoyment or something to help us lose weight- we have stopped looking to understand what nourishment truly means. When you look at your body from a cellular level, you realize that all food has energy and everything that goes into your body does and will influence it.

Nourishment includes food, drink, things that you put on your body and what you breathe. When you begin to think about your body as a machine, you can start to be more mindful of what you put into it. Think about where it comes from, how it was produced, how it was packaged and how long it has been since it was harvested.

Spending more time in this space- you can place attention on enjoying the food that you're eating, preparing/cooking it yourself, growing it and taking part in that process (gardening/farming), and learning about where it has come from in the world.

2. EASTERN/ANCESTRAL INFLUENCES

Eastern/Ancestral Influences relates to all of the different influences that we have had in our lives since before we were born. In this book, I talk a lot about going back to the roots of living and learning from our ancestors- returning to the origin. Whether it is Ayurveda, Traditional Chinese Medicine, herbal medicine or European traditions of fermentation and food preserving- every area of the world has ancestral roots and traditions with food and living. Where do you come from? What is your ethnicity and background- and how did your ancestors live?

It is incredibly helpful to do some research into your background- so that you can begin to understand where you come from, what your body knows and how certain foods may impact your health. This is where local and seasonal really comes into play as well- where you were brought up almost always has an impact on the types of foods your body processes with ease. If you were brought up in a seasonal and cold climate- then it probably doesn't make sense for you to eat tropical fruits all day everyday. Keep in mind, where you currently live also has an impact.

Feeling out of balance? Noticing inflammation and pain in your body? Reach out to one of the amazing resources out there such as massage, herbal medicine, osteopathy or acupuncture- and expand your horizon of healing and living in balance modalities.

3. SENSORY THERAPY

We all have access to more than one sense in our existence. Many of us have all 5 senses and so many of us neglect many of them. I always get so affected by the stories of people who lost their hearing or sight- and then magically (through medicine or natural causes) regained the sense. They are not only in tears, but it is like their level of living is immediately expanded. How many of us take advantage of our senses? When it comes to sensory therapy- it can be anything from playing music, to a blind taste test, to smelling different essential oils. When you separate your senses and focus your attention on one sense, alone, it takes you to another place.

There are so many ways to explore sensory therapy- and some of my favourites are essential oils, colour and chakra therapy as well as singing. I encourage you to find your favourite methods!

4.   ANIMALS & NATURE

Ever since I was a little girl I have been completely obsessed with animals. I have always had animals in my life and I always turn to nature when I am need of some good old grounding therapy. When you think about it- how many children love animals? What is it about animals that children (and people) are so attracted to? In my opinion, the thing about animals and nature is that there is a true presence reflected in them. Animals aren't thinking about their next meeting, money, debt or family problems. Animals are here, now. They are in the present. As is all of nature. So, when we are around animals and in nature- we too feel present. Nature is energizing and represents pure love.

5. WATER

I have no doubt that you know how important water is. If we're not careful, water will be the source of the next world war. Water is completely essential. It is one of those amazing resources that we consume and live with every day of our lives- and as a result, we take complete advantage of it.

We've all heard it "drink more water". With every client I work with, water is the focus of the first conversations we have. Globally, we are not only malnourished (nutrient wise not quantity of food) but we are also dehydrated. Our bodies are constantly working to keep us in balance and keep us alive- and a lot of these processes require water. Each and every single cell in your body is made up of water. Over 70% of your body is water. Your brain is water. Almost every process requires water and not only that but many things we put into our bodies and put our bodies through expends water. Stress, coffee, eating, movement- they all dehydrate us.

When you begin to think about how much water is used in your body, and how much you drink everyday- does it make sense? How many liters of water do you drink everyday?

With water, quantity is not the only important focus to think about. Quality. Water quality is important. Where does your water come from? How was it processed/

filtered? The issues with water are very similar to food. Food is not just food anymore. Some of the things that we call "food" our bodies actually call "toxins" or "garbage". Similarly, not all water is water, to our bodies. There is such thing is dead water. Have you ever heard of the Japanese scientist, Masaru Emoto and his famous water study? If you haven't I highly recommend checking it out. In essence, water is energy and energy is a living matter. When you add chemicals, filter, and remove water from it's natural source- over time it too will lose life. Water has a charge and its quality will effect whether or not it is properly absorbed in your body and whether it actually hydrates you.

6. BREATHING/AIR

You might be noticing a pattern here: water, food, air. All of the natural resources we have in our world that we have taken for granted and lost consciousness about, are actually the three things that are fundamental to our survival. Not only that, they are fundamental to our happiness.

Breathing is a subconscious behavior. We have been breathing throughout our lives without paying attention to it or having to put work into it. Breathing just happens.

The thing about subconscious behavior, is that it can become so disregarded that it can be lost. We don't breath enough. In yoga, subconscious breathing is also referred to as shallow breathing. When you breathe, in order to properly reach every cell in your body and truly nourish your being with oxygen- you need to breathe deeply.

Breathing is also about the quality of air. What air are you breathing: where does it come from, what does it contain and how has it been influenced?

7.   HOME & COMMUNITY

We are social animals. Our communities are important to us and we value our home spaces. This is such an important area for your happiness and for balance. The idea is that home is "where the heart is" and to have this, it's important to put focus into your home and to nourish it. Whether this means spending time in a community that makes you feel good, building a community that you love or beautifying your home- these activities are all an important part of re-balancing and living consciously.

8. TRAVEL/MOVEMENT

Travel and movement are really about the same thing for me. It's about getting outside of your comfort zone, shifting your perspective, experiencing new elements of living and interacting with new energies. You don't need to go on a trip to another country/city for this to happen- although, I do encourage it every now and then.

The idea is to just get uncomfortable.

Go somewhere new.

Try something new.

Move your body in new ways.

Bottom line: get comfortable with being uncomfortable.

9. JOY

These last two pieces really are about the same thing: feeling good and witnessing happiness and gratitude. The idea is to recognize the things that make you happy and that you enjoy- and to do more of it. We all do so much all the time. There is always so much going on- so much noise. A lot of the noise is unnecessary- filling space. So ask yourself, what actually makes you happy? What actually brings you joy and leaves you feeling at peace?

When you think about the concept of expansive and contractive- it becomes even more clear. Expansive relates to feeling alive and free whereas contractive, in opposition, is about feeling constricted, small and energy less. The idea is to bring awareness to what excites you and what drains you. We all get tired and we are all busy but it is possible to spend less time doing for the sake of doing, and more time mindfully focusing on expansive behaviors and actions that we enjoy and which make us feel good.

Ask yourself:

- What do I enjoy?

- What makes me feel good?

- What do I spend my time doing that I don't enjoy and what can I remove from my life that is unnecessary noise and leaves me feeling tired?

10. LOVE

Last and definitely not least- the foundation of it all: love. Love is about recognizing the love within you and also mindfully surrounding yourself with love. Do you spend time in a loving environment/space? Are you surrounded by loving and supportive people? Do you have a community? Do you have a self-love practice and routine that you can turn to when you are out of balance? When you take a deep breath and sit in silence, do you feel love?

The idea with the different spaces, is to explore what these areas mean to you and fill them in based on how you live your life and what influences you are and have been exposed to. When you combine all 10 spaces, you will begin to see that each in their own way, and collectively, come together to nourish each state of your being (mind, body and soul). So, depending on where you are feeling out of "flow" or what is causing your discomfort in the moment, you can choose a space to focus your attention on.

The idea is to get outside of your comfort zone and begin to get exposed to complementary ways of living that will truly bring your mind, body and soul into balance. When you are feeling lost or not yourself, choose one of the 10 spaces to focus on in that day. Engulf yourself in the experience.

For example, spend a day in sensory therapy. Book an essential oil massage, sing your heart out in a group or on your own in nature (or in the shower), spend an hour (or three) in the land of colouring books, attend an aura soma or chakra workshop, and spend an evening with your partner practicing the technique of touch. Expand your sensory horizons and literally, awaken your being.

> ## *When you take a deep breath and sit in silence, do you feel love?*

Once you've dabbled in individual spaces, try your hand at incorporating more than one in a day. Get playful! The idea is to start living, and taking life a little less seriously. Eat the food that you've been craving. Start breathing. Drink water that heals you, instead of harming you. Plant your own food; face your fears of intimacy and sexuality.

Once you begin incorporating this plan into your daily life, I promise your world will expand into one that no longer feels unfamiliar or not worth living. We are complex beings, we are not just our minds, and we are not just our bodies. We spend so much time focusing on one area- and purely neglect the other two. There is no one solution or treatment for anything- we all are special and have unique experiences.

"Dear Human:

You've got it all wrong.

You didn't come here to master unconditional love. This is where you came from and where you'll return.

You came here to learn personal love.

Universal love.

Messy love.

Sweaty Love.

Crazy love.

Broken love.

Whole love.

Infused with divinity.

Lived through the grace of stumbling.

Demonstrated through the beauty of... messing up.

Often.

You didn't come here to be perfect, you already are.

You came here to be gorgeously human. Flawed and fabulous.

And rising again into remembering.

But unconditional love? Stop telling that story.

Love in truth doesn't need any adjectives.

It doesn't require modifiers.

It doesn't require the condition of perfection.

It only asks you to show up.

And do your best.

That you stay present and feel fully.

That you shine and fly and laugh and cry and hurt and heal and fall and get back up and play and work and live and die as YOU.

Its enough.

It's Plenty." — Courtney Walsh

BUILDING A HOLISTIC KITCHEN

Before we get started, the most important thing for you to know is this: Rome was not built in a day. And neither was your kitchen or holistic lifestyle. Transitions and transformations take time, and it's important that you give yourself manageable steps. Otherwise, it's like you're setting out to write, publish and market a book without having any idea of what you are writing about. Before you know it, you're overwhelmed and you give up. We spend so much time thinking about the future and who we want to be, where we want to be and how we want to feel and look– that we scare ourselves out of actually doing and being in that moment. This is when planning can really be more harmful than helpful. You have to start somewhere, and sometimes it's less terrifying you begin here, without a large, outlandish and incredibly attractive vision of where you want to be.

The same goes for your kitchen. Start small. Detoxifying your life and household is a journey and it's important to remember that you have been living this life for (assuming) quite some time, so a quick and timeless change is less than practical.

When it comes to change, figure out what is most important and start there- and let all the other things fall into place, step by step.

Comparison can be a slippery slope (conscious repetition). I know what it's like- you pick up a book or meet or find someone that you look up to and immediately you want his or her life. They seem so happy, healthy and balanced- and you just want that. So you decide that it is your mission to do everything in your power to follow their lifestyle- and before you know it your kitchen no longer looks like yours- and you have no idea what to do with what you've bought. There are so many incredible recipe and health books out there- filled with tips, tools and suggestions on what you need to create a new lifestyle and be a healthy person. A lot of the guides are incredibly similar and list a lot of the same foods (all of which you can buy at Whole Foods). On the one hand, it's wonderful! On the other hand, it takes away the idea of being your own person and really owning your life and your space.

I too am offering you my Holistic Guide, however, I urge you to take this transition step by step and to allow yourself a realistic timeline upon which you begin to use this as a blueprint to create your own lifestyle. Find what works for you, find what you love and find what makes you shine. Not every food I eat is going to be your favourite- and the same right back at me. It's all about trying things out,

experimenting and taking your time. It's about creating a sustainable, livable, lovable and amazing life that you can live...till the end of time!

One of the first places to start when it comes to creating a healthy lifestyle and a holistic home is to identify the foods that your body loves and the foods that you body doesn't desire as much. As a Holistic Nutritionist, this is where I urge you to inquire (if you haven't already) with your body either through your own symptomatology testing, elimination diet or speaking with a Nutritionist or ND- to find out the foods that work for you. Chances are, you are also already quite familiar with this- through living and knowing what foods bug you and what don't.

This relates back to the concept of intuitive eating. When we eat something and our tummy hurts- that is usually an indication that there is imbalance. This is where self-investigation takes place: does it mean you have an intolerance, do you have low stomach acid or high stomach acid, are you experiencing anxiety? This is where the fun begins! You are getting to know your body and re-establishing that beautiful innate connection.

Now a days, there are quite a few common food allergens and intolerances (a result of excessive food processing, pesticides, chemicals and toxins), so it's a lot easier to figure this out on your own. I live a plant-powered lifestyle, meaning that I focus most of my diet around plants. I don't eat any meat and rarely eat dairy. In my experience, a lot of the time food intolerances begin with dairy and gluten. It just so happens that these are the most common food allergens and a lot of it relates back to the idea of excessive food processing. This is something to explore more (in another book).

Ok, I think that we're almost ready to inspire your kitchen and begin creating a space of true nourishment and love. Before we begin, there is one thing that I want to make very clear moving forward, when it comes to your health journey:

Change doesn't happen overnight and neither does building a conscious home and life. Step by step darling, you will get there. Enjoy the journey!

> 66
> # It's about creating a sustainable, livable, lovable and amazing life

If you need to write this on your chalkboard or write it on your fridge- do it. It is so important that we continue to practice self-compassion and to allow time to build a strong and solid foundation. Everything that I practice and teach is basically about moving as far away from the "diet" paradigm as possible and expressing the importance of re-learning how to live. That is what's so funny/absurd about it all; our ancestors knew how to live in balance. Before all of the crazy and upsetting developments of the Industrial Revolution, globalization and the resulting industries (factory farming, over-population, extinction, pollution, etc.) we had

it down when it came to nourishment. People made their own food; local, organic and seasonal were a norm not a privilege and illnesses such as diabetes, obesity, cancer and Alzheimer's were not common household experiences.

So, we are truly bringing it back to the beginning and creating harmony between the ways that we were and the ways that we are now.

Do you remember your grand mothers kitchen? Do you remember what she made, what her cupboards were filled with and the amount of time that she spent in there? Do you remember going grocery shopping with her- where she went and what she bought? Do you remember how much she spent? If you never met your grandparents, ask your parents or your friends about their experiences.

These are all things to bring awareness to when it comes to building a conscious kitchen. We have moved so far away from natural and normal methods of nourishment, that now, it always seems way too complicated to make your own meal or plan for a weeks' worth of meals for a family. It has taken us quite some time to move away from these practices though, so remember to give yourself some time.

CREATING A CONSCIOUS KITCHEN

It's time to offer your kitchen some love. One thing I always do when I move into a new home or even a hotel room- is I personalize my space. Homes are sacred and it's important that you make your home feel, like a home. The same goes for your kitchen. Do you like your kitchen? Does your kitchen make you feel good and inspired? Do you feel anxious when you enter your kitchen, worried about bingeing on your old favourite snacks? These are all things to begin thinking about when it comes to creating a holistic and conscious space. Add some of you into your kitchen (flowers, pictures, quotes, letters and cards on the fridge, speakers, cookbooks).

A conscious kitchen also speaks to whether or not it has flow. Is your kitchen practical? Can you reach ingredients, are your shelves organized, do you know where everything is, do you have items that you need? The idea is to create a space that you not only enjoy being in but that also makes creating fun food and simple.

To start this process, the first thing to do is to personalize and organize your kitchen. So let's get to it:

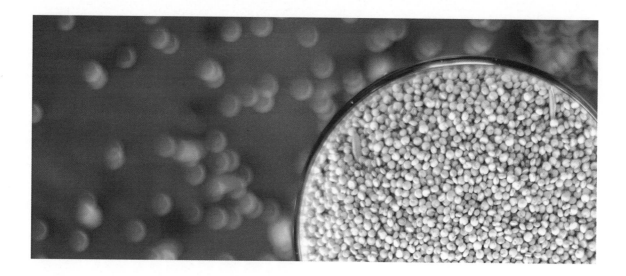

1.   CLEARING SPACE

Just like cleaning out your closet or doing a full house clean, organizing your
kitchen starts with a solid clear out. Empty out your cupboards, pantry, drawers,
fridge and freezer. You won't know what you have and what you are missing- until
you go through this step. Also, nothing feels better than just pulling it all out and
creating a bit of chaos; even if it's for a mere moment. If you're up to it, light some
incense, burn sage or palo santo or use an essenttial oil diffuser - clear the energy.

2.   CLEAR IT OUT – WHAT DON'T YOU NEED

This is definitely one of my favourite steps. Just get rid of it. Whether you
choose to throw it away, recycle it, or give it to someone- that is up to you. My
recommendation when it comes to all the junk is to just get rid of it. Detoxify your
kitchen. Bid farewell to all the junk, processed and refined foods and things that are
expired and rotten. This includes old and processed dressings and sauces. Things
that you haven't used in years- throw them away. Remember, not only do these
things hold up space but they also offer the invitation to consume them. If it's not
there you won't consume it.

3. CLEAR IT OUT - OLD ITEMS

Much like purging old foods and products, the same goes for storage containers and tupperware. Get rid of things that have missing lids or are damaged. Get rid of utensils that don't match. Keep in mind that everything in your kitchen space should be there for a reason. Everything holds energy and you want to start feeling fresh and full of intention.

4. CLEANING

Now that you've removed all unwanted things- you can clean. Scrub your cupboards and fridge/freezer, get rid of dust and wipe down all surfaces. Remember to use eco-friendly cleaning products (paraben-free).

5. ORGANIZE

Every controlling person's favourite task: organize. Now you begin to put everything back, intentionally, in their place. Make things pretty. Put things in places based on accessibility: what do you use all the time and need easy access to?

BUYING ORGANIC FOOD

The Clean 15 & Dirty Dozen Rule of Thumb

You may have heard of this already. You may not have. Basically, when you are just starting out in familiarizing yourself with the food industry, and the organic industry in particular- you will learn a lot about the ways that food is produced, harvested and treated in the world. What it comes down to is that there is a lot that goes into mass market food that we do not always know about, and a lot of the fresh produce that you are buying contains many harmful and toxic pesticides and herbicides that you cannot just wash away. Although knowing that something is 'organic' isn't a global stamp of approval that ensures that your food is clean and 100% good for you- it is definitely a great place to start.

When you are looking into buying organic, you are also moving away from the entire GMO (genetically modified) or GE (genetically engineered) movement and chances are- your food has been produced and grown in a much more ethical and careful manner. The standards of organic are very strict, globally, and it takes a lot for a farmer to have their products become organic certified. So, it does mean something. Also, it absolutely costs a lot more to grow organically, and to get the certification. So, you are paying for more.

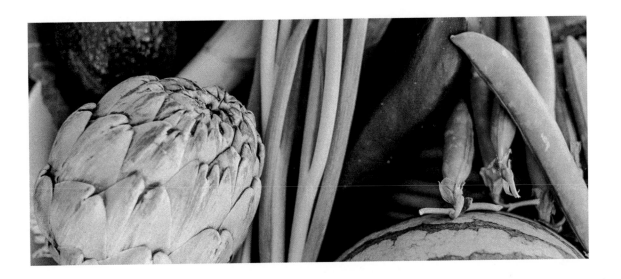

This entire topic could be a book on it's own, which is why the Clean 15, Dirty Dozen list was created in the first place. It was introduced by the Environmental Working Group to offer the general public a rule of thumb when it comes to buying produce. Since their first list was released, they have continued with updated versions annually, in addition to a lot of supplementary information (available through their website) on pesticides, effects, the industry, etc., as well as an annual report. I highly recommend that you check it out at some point, and spend some time reading all about the food that you eat on the regular.

For now, let's keep it simple and stick to the Clean 15 and the Dirty Dozen. The most recent report (2015) includes the following in each list:

CLEAN 15:

Avocados	Onions	Eggplant
Sweet Corn	Asparagus	Grapefruit
Pineapples	Mangos	Cantaloupe
Cabbage	Papayas	Cauliflower
Sweet peas frozen	Kiwi	Sweet Potatoes

DIRTY DOZEN:

Apples	Celery	Hot Peppers
Peaches	Sweet Bell Peppers	Kale/Collard Greens
Nectarines	Cucumbers	
Strawberries	Cherry Tomatoes	
Grapes	Snap Peas- imported	
Spinach	Potatoes	

If you are out shopping, and don't have access to the list or forget (which is perfectly understandable and happens to me all the time), a great way to estimate the list is to remember the following:

- if the fruit/veg has a thick skin that you remove prior to consuming it, chances are, it will be on the clean 15 (more often than not).

- fruits and vegetable that are high in sugar tend to be on the dirty dozen. The reason being, they are sprayed more because of their high sugar/fructose content.

*If you want to take it a step further? Know your farmers, educate yourself on local farming and buy directly from them.

CONSUMING RIPE PRODUCE

Another great rule of thumb when it comes to buying produce and nutrition. If you are exposed to the vegan/plant-based community at all, you may have seen an active vegan walking around with an extremely large bag or box of very, very ripe bananas. Why are they doing this? The reason why buying ripe produce is beneficial is because the more ripe the fruit, the more nutritional it is. This entire concept relates to mother nature. Unfortunately, in the food industry, it is normal to harvest fruits before they are ready to consume. A large part of this is shelf-life and the bottom-line, money. If you were out in nature though, you know that fruit is ready when it drops off the tree or falls off the plant. A fruit is "ready" when it has properly bloomed and it's nutrients are properly developed and bio-available. So whether you buy the fruit and vegetables before hand and wait for them to ripen, or buy them ripe to freeze or eat- if you are looking to get the best nutrition from your food, consuming them at prime ripeness is key.

YOUR SHOPPING LIST

Make a Shopping List for any must haves you are missing for your pantry:

PLANT BASED SUBSTITUTIONS

Dairy Milk

- ☐ Nut mylks: almond, cashew, coconut, hazelnut, walnut
- ☐ Seed mylks: hemp, sunflower, pumpkin

Cheese

- ☐ Vegan cheese (nut & seed based)
- ☐ Nutritional yeast

Meat

- ☐ Tempeh
- ☐ Organic Soy, Tofu

OILS TO START

- ☐ Coconut Oil (for cooking)
- ☐ Extra Virgin Olive Oil (for Dressings)

- ☐ Sesame Oil
- ☐ Other acceptable oils: Flax Oil, hemp oil, avocado oil

PANTRY ITEMS

- ☐ Cans of coconut Milk
- ☐ Apple cider vinegar
- ☐ Miso paste
- ☐ Desiccated coconut
- ☐ Organic Corn Tortilla Chips
- ☐ Gluten free Pastas

- ☐ Vegetable Stock for Soups
- ☐ Rice/buckwheat Crackers
- ☐ Organic Popcorn
- ☐ Garlic
- ☐ Onions
- ☐ Yams or Sweet potatoes

- ☐ Lentils
- ☐ Chickpeas
- ☐ Nuts and seeds
- ☐ Tea
- ☐ Coconut oil
- ☐ Granola
- ☐ Quinoa

FRESH PRODUCE STAPLES

- ☐ Greens: spinach, kale, arugul, chard, romaine
- ☐ Mushrooms: brown crimini, shitake, Portobello,
- ☐ Broccoli
- ☐ Cauliflower
- ☐ Celery Root
- ☐ Celery
- ☐ Leeks
- ☐ Onions
- ☐ Carrots
- ☐ Cucumbers
- ☐ Tomatoes
- ☐ Eggplant
- ☐ Bell Peppers
- ☐ Fruit: apples, pineapple, berries, avocado
- ☐ Zucchini

NUTS AND SEEDS   select a minimum of 4-5 variations – YOUR faves, avoiding ones with allergies of course

- ☐ Hemp Seeds
- ☐ Chia seeds
- ☐ Pumpkin seeds
- ☐ Sunflower Seeds
- ☐ Sesame Seeds
- ☐ Cashews
- ☐ Walnuts
- ☐ Almonds
- ☐ Pecans

GLUTEN FREE GRAINS   Select 3 or 4 to start

- ☐ Quinoa
- ☐ Amaranth
- ☐ Jasmine or Basmati Rice
- ☐ Kasha, Soba or Couscous
- ☐ Buckwheat Groats
- ☐ Rolled oats
- ☐ Steel cut oats

ACCEPTABLE FLOURS

- ☐ Brown Rice Flour
- ☐ Coconut Flour
- ☐ Buckwheat Flour
- ☐ Quinoa Flour

STAPLE SEASONINGS

- ☐ Sea Salt
- ☐ Himalayan Salt
- ☐ Rosemary
- ☐ Cumin
- ☐ Turmeric
- ☐ Cinnamon
- ☐ Cardamom
- ☐ Cayenne, Chilli
- ☐ Black Pepper
- ☐ Paprika
- ☐ Nutmeg
- ☐ Vanilla

CONDIMENTS/REFRIGERATOR STAPLES

- ☐ Organic Ketchup
- ☐ Apple Cider Vinegar
- ☐ Balsamic Vinegar
- ☐ Dijon Mustard
- ☐ Wheat Free Tamari or Nama Shoyu
- ☐ Hummus
- ☐ Almond Butter
- ☐ Tahini (sesame seed butter)
- ☐ Fresh Lemons/Limes
- ☐ Fresh Ginger Root
- ☐ Sauerkraut
- ☐ Miso Paste

ACCEPTABLE SWEETENERS

- ☐ Honey (Unpasteurized, Local Preferred)
- ☐ Maple Syrup
- ☐ Dates
- ☐ Raisins
- ☐ Figs
- ☐ Stevia (NO Glycemic Index– Suitable for Diabetics)
- ☐ Brown Rice Syrup

SUPERFOODS

- ☐ Cacao
- ☐ Ashwaganda
- ☐ `Superfoods: chaga, reishi, lions mane
- ☐ Maca
- ☐ Chia Seeds
- ☐ Spirulina (or E3Live Brand)
- ☐ Schizandra berry powder
- ☐ Moringa Powder
- ☐ Matcha Powder

ACCEPTABLE BEVERAGES

- Sparkling Perrier Water
- Herbal Teas of Choice (chamomile, mint, ginger, dandelion root)
- Organic coffee
- Matcha green tea powder
- Homemade iced tea

EQUIPMENT

- Spring form pan (raw and vegan baking/desserts)
- Cutting boards
- Quality knives
- Pots
- Pans
- Blender
- Measuring cups
- Lemon juicer
- Grater/zester
- Tupperwares
- Fabric bags
- Nut milk bag
- Bottle opener
- Blender
- Hand Blender
- Food processor
- Strainer
- Can opener
- Mason jars

CHLOE'S 15 KITCHEN STAPLES

- Nuts & Seeds
- Tahini
- Tamari
- Olive Oil
- Coconut Oil
- Turmeric
- Cumin
- Sea Salt
- Clean water
- Greens
- Quinoa
- Legumes
- Fresh Fruit
- Cayenne
- Tea

BATCH COOKING AND STOCKING YOUR FREEZER

I told you that I was going to tell you my secrets, and here they are. It's pretty simple- most Holistic Nutritionist's and health practitioners are big fans and followers of the batch cooking and freezing movement. This practice will literally change your life. There is a small element of planning that comes into play- and the idea is that when you begin to create a set of recipes and meals that are your go-to's, you can gradually decrease the amount of time and effort you spend thinking and planning food. Like anything, it just requires putting in some extra effort in the beginning- to reap the delicious benefits later.

When it comes to batch cooking, the idea is that you designate 1 day of out the week where you set yourself up for the rest of the week. Most people love Sundays for this- because it already tends to be a day of errands and planning for the week. The idea is that on that day, you take your list to the grocery store, grab your items, head home and spend a few hours in the kitchen, preparing meals and ingredients that will be your lunches, breakfast' and dinners for the rest of the week. The amount that you prepare for is up to you, and also varies depending on what your week looks like (do you have meetings, dinner, events, social plans, etc. to work around).

The amazing news is that many items that you batch-cook can be frozen and will last for several weeks (to even months), which is a huge time saver. I always have a selection of raw desserts in my freezer so that whenever we are craving something comforting and delicious- we can satisfy that craving with something incredibly delicious and nutritious and then, the craving is gone and you can move on with your life (without guilt, fear, anxiety, etc.).

WHAT CAN YOU BATCH COOK?

Raw Vegetables

- wash and grate carrots, beets, squash, zucchini

Soak & Cook Grains and Legumes:

- Quinoa
- Rice
- Chickpeas
- Black beans
- Lentils

Greens

- wash and chop greens
- wash and chop herbs

Dressings

- Make your dressings for the week

Roasted Vegetables

- Roast beets, pumpkin, squash, and seasonal vegetables

Smoothie packages

- Place greens, frozen fruit, nut mylk cubes, greens powder in a ziplock bag ready to grab and blend

WHAT CAN YOU FREEZE?

- Soups
- Raw Desserts
- Superfood balls/truffles
- Raw Chocolates
- Energy Bars
- Fruit
- Smoothie packages
- Juices
- Nut mylks

Freezing tip: if you are freezing glass, leave an inch at the tip and freeze without the lid first to avoid messy explosions.

CHLOE'S FAVOURITE SUPERFOOD BALLS

INGREDIENTS:

1 cup	almonds
1 cup	dates (pitted, chopped)
¾ cup	desiccated coconut
1 tbsp	maple syrup
1 tbsp	spirulina powder
pinch	himalayan salt
1 tsp	cinnamon
1 tsp	vanilla powder or extract

Desiccated coconut for rolling

HOW TO:

Grind nuts and dates in a food processor or blender.

Transfer to a medium bowl and add the coconut, salt, vanilla, cinnamon and spirulina and mix with your hands, compressing together. Gradually add in maple syrup and continue mixing together.

Roll into individual balls and roll in the desiccated coconut.

Store in an airtight container in the fridge for 3 weeks or in the freezer for 6 months+.

SOAKING LEGUMES, SEEDS, NUTS

Have you heard about soaking, sprouting and activated nuts and seeds? The truth is, this is an important step when it comes to optimal nutrition and digestion. It's not bogus. In fact, these methods come from ancient traditions and have been practiced amongst many cultures, groups and societies throughout history.

The reasoning behind soaking your grains, legumes, nuts and seeds is that these ingredients all contain anti-nutrients, specifically phytates and enzyme inhibitors, which detract from their optimal nutritional value and bind up the minerals so your body is unable to absorb them properly.

The idea is to soak the grain, nuts and seeds in filtered water for a particular amount of time. Each product has varying directions with regards to time and method. It helps to do some research on your most used item, and become a master (hint: google is your friend).

FOOD PHOTOGRAPHY: THE STORY

I can't believe that I am a food photographer. I can't believe that I get paid to take photos of food. If you told me that I would be doing that when I was younger, I would've cringed and called you crazy. Me, taking pictures of food as a job. Insanity. Amazing!

I remember always paying attention to the Yearbook team in high school and feeling envious that they got to take photos of things all day. I almost found it such an outlandish thing to do- that I wrote it off as unrealistic. However, when I pay attention to my thoughts and experiences through the years, it becomes clear to me that photography was always something I was curious about. In university, a few of my friends got into photography and splurged to buy themselves nice cameras- and again, I sort of cast it aside as something unrealistic. So much so, that I never asked to use the camera or try it out- I just ignored it. I was always a subject.

This all changed when I started Chloe's Countertop. Suddenly, I needed nice photos to accompany my writing. I couldn't just write. As I was nearing the end of my education to become a Holistic Nutritionist, and my love for food and health was in full development- the time spent in my kitchen cooking and snapping photos increased.

I'll never forget one of the first photos I posted on Instagram- it was the beginning of spring and I was walking my dog Ollie just outside my apartment building on West Georgia Street in Vancouver. For the first time in months, I noticed these beautiful bright pink flowers blooming just outside the concierge of my building- in bushes I never had glanced at twice previously. There they were, stunning, begging to be captured.

I took the photo, not completely sure of why or what I was going to do with it. I

had a small and silent idea though, Instagram. Standing outside, feeling the tug of Ollie's leash, as he wondered what on earth I could be up to during his ritual afternoon walk- I began the practice that would soon become second nature. I truly had no idea what I was doing- what filters to use, what was saturation, brightness and contrast. I didn't know anything about photography and I surely had no concept of art or creativity, I thought. Something beyond my critical mind directed this behavior though. And I posted it. This doesn't end with thousands of likes and 1 million followers in ten minutes. In fact, I probably didn't get anymore than 10 likes (all of which were my friends). But, I remember it so clearly. That was the beginning of something new and beautiful in my life. And I truly had no concept or idea of it.

I'm telling this story because I want to show you, through my own experiences, that you don't always have to know what you are doing, while you do it. You may have absolutely no reason, concept or understanding. Sometimes you just have to do it, because there is something deep and well beyond the rational mind that is telling you to, to move forward, to take the jump. This can be as little as taking a photo or as big as signing up for a yoga teacher training class or holistic nutritionist certification. Something that may or may not change your life. Maybe it's a move, maybe it's ending a relationship, maybe it's the food that you feared all these years. I don't know your story. What I do know, is that it will, at the very least, change the course of it.

When it comes to food photography, there are a few major focuses to keep in mind- at least when you are first getting started and learning how to create your own style and theme. As with anything to do with branding and business, it is important to create your own style and a look that is unique to you and your brand. The way to design this is to work around what you like.

A FEW QUESTIONS TO BEGIN ASKING YOURSELF WHEN YOU'RE STARTING OUT INCLUDE:

- What are you drawn to?

- What colours and styles catch your eye?

- Do you like neutral colours or more extreme?

- Do you prefer a more natural look, or more composed?

- What editing style are you attracted to?

- Do you prefer zoomed in, or zoomed out?

- Do you like more or less detail?

- Do you enjoy accessories in the shot or more minimalist?

- What backgrounds do you like (wood, modern, rustic, clean)

These are all things to begin thinking about. Chances are, when you scroll through your Instagram and Pinterest accounts- you will notice a few trends and patterns. Become more conscious of these things when you start preparing your food and taking pictures- what are you most focused on.

To introduce you to Food Photography- I have created 6 spaces of interest and steps to organize your thoughts. You do not need to be a professional or professionally trained to appreciate and get started with these steps. They are merely tools to focus your attention and to begin building your repertoire of photography style.

To get started, I want to encourage you to look at yourself as a photographer (or whatever vocation you are interested in). Just because you are not being paid for it, and you don't promote yourself as that- the idea is to put more positive energy towards what you are doing. We so often put ourselves down and set unrealistic expectations of what we need to do or how we're doing. I never looked at myself as a photographer, until I started receiving offers for jobs- that was when I realised that I am looked at as a photographer. So own it! You have the potential to do and be anything you want- you just have to choose to believe it.

1.   SETTING:

It all starts with setting. Where are you taking your photos? What does your studio space look like? It's important to choose a setting that is clean, is exposed to natural light and that you have access to at all times. Also, make sure that

- Choose your setting

- Simple and plain backgrounds

- Use plates/backgrounds/tablecloths with colours that contrast or harmonize with your food- not the same colour

- Make sure everything is in the shot for a reason, remove any clutter (stray people, cutlery)

2. LIGHT

When you speak to a photographer chances are they will tell you that the number one thing to be mindful of is light. Natural light is a photographer's best friend. This fact remains true with food photography, and in some cases, more so. Natural light is crucial to beautiful photography. There is nothing like an artificially lit photo of breakfast (at night-time). It just never does the food justice (believe me, I've been there and done that).

I realize that sometimes you have no choice and you can't wait (or it's dinner time and you can't let it sit overnight) but if you can help it- really value your natural light with food photography.

My favourite thing to do is have my photo "spot" or photo studio in my apartment where all of my things are (tripod, camera, accessories and backdrops) and that is the best spot in the house for natural light.

Get well acquainted with the natural light in your home- it will be your best friend. Indirect natural light is best.

- Get comfortable with what angels work and the different settings on your camera to complement these styles

3. SHOOT A LOT (ANGLES, ZOOMS, DIFFERENT ACCESSORIES)

The best way to get better and to learn is to do it a lot. When I first started out, I would spend hours each day shooting food. Everyone has their favourite angel, frame and style and the best way to find out what is yours, is to try many different kinds. Shoot all over your apartment/home, use different colours, backgrounds and textures and soon you will find what your eye enjoys most (and what your customers love too).

- Get used to what your style is

- Different angles work for different foods and light

- Down low, head on, high up- geometry of presentation

4.   COLOUR BALANCE

White balance when it comes to food phtography is super important because it determines how we correctly see the colours in the image based on what the actual eye sees in real-life. Cameras capture colour based on what type of light is being used to light the scene. It is important that you know how to change the white balance setting on your camera- based on the type of light you are using in your shoot. So, for instance, with natural or sunlight you use the daylight or sunny white balance. This relates to not only getting to know your camera but also noticing the type of light you are working with on any given day.

- Most important when natural light isn't available when you can have a yellow or blue cast- use white balance setting on camera or edit digitally

5. ZOOM IN

This is of course, a matter of preference. However, I would say that it is important that you are mindful of what you are including in the shot. If you are solely focusing on the food, make sure to fill your frame with the food (and whatever details you are including). There is nothing like taking a set of photos to later realize that the plate was dirty or you accidentally forgot to remove an element from the frame. Be mindful.

- Based on your style, helps to amplify taste, texture, deliciousness

- Fill the frame with the food

6. PREPARATION

Dependent upon the type of food photographer that you are, it may be helpful to include photos of your preparation process. This is especially important if you are food blogger or if you intend on posting the recipe somewhere online or in print. This is where it can get interesting- if you are doing preparation shots, chances are you will have to be slightly more meticulous and clean than you would if you didn't take these shots. Again, keep in mind that all of these mentioned points are still important.

7.   DETAILS

Food photography is all about the details, especially when you are taking macro shots. Plan out your frame, make sure that all of your elements are clean and tidy and that everything is there for a reason. Use things like drizzled olive oil and water to help enhance the food to make them styled fresh and bright.

- Keep your props and elements clean

- Choose fresh ingredients

- Highlight Colour and texture

- Keep it simple

- Use simple props (raw ingredients, favorite accessories)

- Add a human element

- Add a drizzle of olive oil to enhance freshness

LIVING A RECIPE-LESS LIFE

So here it is. The juice. After a lot of meditation, experience, challenge, living and tribulations I have come to realize the following truth. Life is here to be lived without a recipe. What do I mean by this? You don't need to follow a plan.

So much of life is spent wondering if what we are doing is right. Am I a success or a failure? Am I doing this wrong? We spend so much time in our heads, wondering if what we are doing is good or bad, acceptable or unacceptable. When you take a step back and pay attention to the amount of time that is dedicated to this action of evaluating and judging what you're doing, it becomes pretty clear why life isn't always feeling totally blissed out. We love to create stories around what we're doing, and dramatizing why they're happening. I'm mad because of this. I'm not feeling great today because of this. So many reasons, so many thoughts.

So why do we judge? Why can't we just do and be, no matter what? This is where our minds become a tool that may not be as helpful as we like to think. Control is restrictive. It limits us to only one way of living. What happens when things don't go our way? When suddenly something happens that wasn't planned for, or you weren't

told about? Usually, this is where chaos and anxiety ensues. Suddenly, you have lost control and you don't know which way to turn. This is what happens when you begin to live a recipe-less life. When you begin to let go of the rules and blueprints and you surrender to the possibility of "fucking up".

The best way I can think to illustrate this is with food. In the foodie world, there tends to be two types of "chefs"; the 'intuitive' chef and the 'baker'. The difference between these two types of chefs is whether or not they follow a recipe when they are creating. When you follow a recipe, you are generally given a guideline and you know how it is supposed to turn out. Aka you know the outcome. An intuitive chef, on the other hand, tends to not follow a recipe and has no idea what the outcome is meant to be. Now, when it comes to cooking- I appreciate that sometimes the baking type is needed, especially with regards to traditional baking. However, when it comes to life- the baking type is limited.

Think about it: how would life feel if you knew the outcome? If you knew exactly what was going to happen, how it was going to happen and what the end would look like? Would you be present to life, or would you pay so much attention to each moment- making sure that it was in-line with that picture, or try to control it so you could change that picture? Either way, chances are- you would be living in the future. Although this sounds ok, the issue is that if you are living in the future you are not fully present in the here and now. Meaning, you cannot possibly truly experience what is here. It's all about being mindful.

Let's think about this in terms of meditation.

FIVE MINUTE MEDITATION:

Grab your phone or a timer and set it to 5 minutes.

Sit down in a comfortable seat, legs folded, arms resting on your thighs, palms faced open and outward. Connect your thumb and pointer finger together and breath. Make sure that you are sitting in a position that is comfortable and where you can sit in silence without moving or fidgeting for a few minutes.

Breath in for 1, 2, 3, 4 seconds. Hold.
Breath out for 1, 2, 3, 4 seconds. Hold.

Breath in for 1, 2, 3, 4 seconds. Hold.
Breath out for 1, 2, 3, 4 seconds. Hold.

Breath in for 1, 2, 3, 4 seconds. Hold.
Breath out for 1, 2, 3, 4 seconds. Hold.

Breath in for 1, 2, 3, 4 seconds. Hold.
Breath out for 1, 2, 3, 4 seconds. Hold.

Continue this sequence until the timer goes.

Where did your mind go? Where did your attention go? Were you focused on your breath or did you think about what you were going to eat for lunch today, breakfast tomorrow or dinner tonight? Did your mind start to wander off, wondering what you did yesterday and wishing that you did something differently? Or perhaps it came to right here, in this moment, and thought about why you weren't better at meditation.

Wherever your mind went- it's helpful to pay attention to your patterns and where your thoughts go when you zone out or get uncomfortable. This should be an indication to the way that you live your life. Do you get anxious? Do you feel silent? Do you feel peace?

When it comes to living a recipe-less life, the idea is that this sort of practice becomes more natural and less of a struggle. Over time, your mind's patterns of going into the future or stepping back into the past becomes a lot less frequent and lot less powerful. When you begin to live your life based on what you are feeling in the moment you will begin to live in more flow. Your actions won't be dependent on what you did yesterday and they won't be determined by what you want to do tomorrow.

You will eat chocolate because your body craves chocolate and not because you woke up late, had a difficult discussion with your partner last night or felt sad about a decision you made yesterday. You will go for a run because you feel like moving, not because you "over-ate" yesterday and feel guilty and worried about getting fat today.

MY MOMENT OF TRANSPARENCY:

I experience resistance when it comes to giving out recipes. This isn't because I am a recipe hoarder or because I don't like sharing my food with others. It's because I don't actually follow recipes myself. Don't get me wrong I absolutely love cookbooks and love buying beautiful cookbooks. I love flipping through recipes and getting inspired. However, the truth is that a lot of my inspiration comes from the photos and just glancing at the ingredients. I tend to steer clear of quantities of each ingredient and even pay little attention to the method of the recipe.

I realize this isn't common amongst everyone, however you would be surprised by how many cookbook authors and food bloggers are just like this. So many people out there don't actually write down recipes, and rely on their memory and experience when it comes to sharing the recipe or publishing it in a cookbook.

I think a lot of this reliance on recipes comes from a fear or lack of confidence with food and in the kitchen. Which is a direct reflection of the way we live our life. We, as a society, have moved so far away from the traditions of our ancestors. Time and time again I am shocked by how many people have little to no experience when it comes to making their own food. Eating out for every meal is more often than not, the norm. There's nothing wrong with eating out (in fact, there's a lot right with it) however, I feel upset when I find out that someone is unable to make themselves their own food.

Eating is instinctual. We all need to eat. It is a part of survival. So what are you going to do if you lose access to restaurants, cafes and food trucks. What if you are given ingredients and the means to cook- and you don't know how to move forward. What if there is no recipe book?

This is where my mission comes in. I want to inspire more people to live a recipe-less life. To cook, eat, and live without rules, guidelines or instructions. To trust themselves, their bodies and their intuition. Somewhere, deep inside your being, lies the ability to cook intuitively. We all have intuition. Yes, some of us may be better equipped or more in-tune, but fear not, you do have an intuition. You are no different.

So try it out. Without following a recipe, take yourself to a grocery store or farmers market, and let your being be your guide. Let your body be your method. Choose the ingredients that call you, head to your kitchen and see what you make.

Let go of the idea of failing. If there is no such thing as failure, then you are not faced with this fear. Then you can just be and do. In fact you may even succeed. Imagine what you would do if you didn't have a fear of failure. How many more things would you do?

So try it out.

Carve your own path.

Let go of your plan.

And live a recipe-less life.

*Note: I have included recipes in this book because they are my faovurites and I've been meaning to share them with you for quite some time. My intention is that you will be inspired by the photography, you will glance at the ingredients and you will challenge yourself to adapt these recipes to your tastes, enjoy them in different ways based on what's locally and seasonally available and they will inspire you to create your own recipes. Enjoy!

THE RECIPES

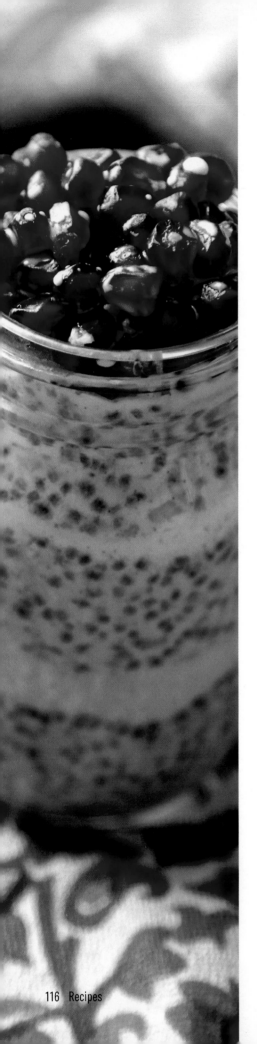

BREAKFAST

SMOOTHIES

DAIRY-FREE MYLKS

HOLISTIC LATTES

chloe's
COUNTERTOP

SAUCES & DRESSINGS

SALADS

SOUPS

chloe's COUNTERTOP

HOLISTIC MAKEOVERS

DESSERTS

Breakfast

OVERNIGHT OATS + STRAWBERRY CASHEW CREAM

chloe's
COUNTERTOP

OVERNIGHT OATS +
STRAWBERRY CASHEW CREAM

serves 2

INGREDIENTS:

1 cup   rolled oats

1 tsp   cinnamon

1 tsp   vanilla

2   cinnamon sticks

1 tbsp   maca powder

favourite dried fruit:
banana chips, dried
cherries, raisins, figs, dates

favourite nuts: hazelnuts,
almonds, walnuts

2 tbsp hemp seeds

2 ½ cups almond mylk

STRAWBERRY CREAM:

½ cup cashews, soaked

1 lemon, zest and juice

1 tbsp raw honey or maple
syrup

¼ cup almond mylk

1 tsp vanilla

1 tsp cinnamon

1 cup fresh strawberries

2 ½ cups almond mylk

HOW TO:

Place all oatmeal ingredients into a mason jar
along with the almond mylk and allow it to sit
overnight or for at least 5 hours

In the morning, place oats in a pot and heat on
low-medium heat for around 20 minutes, stirring
every 5 minutes

In the meantime, place all strawberry cream
ingredients into blender and blend on high (use
tamper to scrape sides) for 2 minutes.

Serve oatmeal in a bowl with grated apple and a
scoop of the strawberry cashew cream.

Mix before eating to ensure delicious creaminess.

chloe's
COUNTERTOP

FIG & TAHINI QUINOA PORRIDGE

INGREDIENTS:

½ cup	quinoa, cooked
2 tbsp	raw tahini
1 tsp	chaga
1 tsp	maca powder
1 tbsp	raspberry chia jam
3	fresh figs, sliced
1 tsp	cinnamon

HOW TO:

Soak, and cook quinoa ahead of time.

Add tahini, maca and chaga and mix together.

Top with chia raspberry jam, cinnamon and fresh figs

RAW ENERGY BARS

Makes 9-12 Bars

INGREDIENTS:

1 cup	nuts (almonds, cashews, walnuts)
1 cup	seeds (sunflower, pumpkin, hemp)
½ cup	desiccated coconut
1 cup	dates
3 tbsp	almond butter OR salted cashew butter
4 tbsp	raw cacao powder
½ cup	chia seeds
1 tsp	cinnamon

HOW TO:

Grind nuts, seeds, and coconut into a fine meal in blender or food processor. Add the dates, almond/salted cashew butter, cinnamon and raw cacao – blend. Move mixture into a bowl, add chia seeds and mix together with your hands. Roll into balls for superfood balls OR place in a baking pan (lined with parchment paper). Place into the freezer. Slice into squares when desired. Lasts in the freezer for 6+ months or the fridge for 3 weeks.

chloe's COUNTERTOP

VANILLA CARDAMOM BANANA PANCAKES

VANILLA CARDAMOM BANANA PANCAKES

INGREDIENTS:

½ cup	buckwheat flour
2 tbsp	chia (4 tbsp water)
1	ripe banana
½ cup	coconut mylk
1 tsp	cardamom
1/2	lemon, juiced & zested
1 tsp	vanilla powder
1 tsp	coconut oil
1 tsp	cinnamon
4 tbsp	filtered water

TOPPING:

1 tbsp desiccated coconut

½ tbsp lemon zest

HOW TO:

Combine chia seeds with 4 tbsp of water and leave to sit in the fridge for about of 30 minutes, or until it becomes a thick gelatinous consistency.

Mash the ripe banana in a bowl and then add it to the blender, along with all of the ingredients.

In a non-stick pan at a medium heat, add the coconut oil and spread it across the pan. Add about ¼ cup of the mix into the pan and treat it like a regular pancake. Once it starts to bubble, flip it to cook for about another minute on the other side. Repeat this step until you are finished with the batter.

Quickly prepare your chocolate tahini orange sauce and raspberry chia jam. Serve your stack of pancakes with these two sauces drizzled on top, and sprinkled with desiccated coconut.

CLASSIC CHIA PUDDING

serves 2

INGREDIENTS:

4 tbsp   Chia Seeds

2 tbsp   desiccated coconut

1 tsp   cinnamon

1 tsp   vanilla

1 ½ cups Almond mylk

HOW TO:

Combine all ingredients into a jar or container, mix (or shake) and leave in the fridge overnight or for at least 30 minutes. Add extra almond mylk if needed when serving, and top with your favourite toppings:

Fresh fruit (blueberries, raspberries, strawberries, grated apple), dried fruit (figs, dates, raisins, cranberries), nuts, seeds (hemp, pumpkin), cacao nibs or granola.

chloe's COUNTERTOP

Smoothies

BANANA COFFEE SHAKE

serves 2

INGREDIENTS:

1	banana (frozen, ripe)	1 cup	almond mylk
3 tbsp	hemp seeds	1 tbsp	almond butter
1 tbsp	coconut oil	1 tbsp	maca powder
½ cup	freshly brewed coffee	1 tsp	cinnamon
		⅛ tsp	cardamom
		1 tsp	vanilla
		2	medjool dates

HOW TO:

Combine all ingredients into your high-speed blender, blend until smooth
and creamy (20 seconds)

GREEN MINT CHOCOLATE
CHIP SMOOTHIE serves 2

INGREDIENTS:

3	frozen bananas
2	medjool dates, pitted
1 tbsp	maca powder
3 cups	of almond or coconut mylk
1 tsp	cinnamon
1 tsp	vanilla
½ cup	spinach
½ tsp	peppermint essential oil

handful of fresh mint leaves
without stems

2 tbsp	raw cacao nibs

optional:

1 tbsp	raw cacao powder

HOW TO:

Add all ingredients into blender and blend on high.

Sprinkle cacao nibs on top.

chloe's
COUNTERTOP

MATCHA GREEN SMOOTHIE BOWL

serves 1

INGREDIENTS:

2 tsp	matcha powder
1 cup	almond mylk
2	dates
1 cup	fresh pineapple
2	frozen bananas
½ cup	fresh or frozen kale (packed in)
1 tsp	maca
1 tsp	cinnamon
1 tsp	vanilla

HOW TO:

Blend all ingredients on high and top with raw granola and coconut in a bowl

TOPPINGS:

crushed raw almonds

desiccated coconut

chia raspberry jam

chia seeds

holistic truffle powder: maca, lucuma, carob, stevia, cinnamon, vanilla, himalayan salt

chloe's
COUNTERTOP

BEET BERRY SMOOTHIE serves 1

INGREDIENTS:

1	roasted or raw beet
1 ½ cup	frozen berries
1	frozen banana
1 cup	almond mylk
1 tsp	maca
1 tsp	cinnamon

HOW TO:

Blend on high and top with raw granola and coconut

CHLOE'S GREEN SMOOTHIE serves 1

INGREDIENTS:

½   avocado
(optional: add the pit of the
avocado to support optimal
digestion)

1   apple

1   piece of ginger
          root

juice of ½ lime

juice of ½ lemon

1 cup   greens
          (kale/spinach)

1 ½ cup filtered water

½   large cucumber

HOW TO:

Add all ingredients into blender and blend on high.

Dairy-free Mylks

LAVENDER ALMOND MYLK

CREAMY HEMP MYLK

Creates just under 1 litre

INGREDIENTS:

1 cup	hemp hearts
3 ½ cups	filtered water
1 tsp	cinnamon
1 tsp	vanilla
1 tbsp	maca powder
½ tbsp	maple syrup
½ tbsp	coconut butter
1 pinch	Himalayan salt

HOW TO:

Add all ingredients into blender and blend on high.

LAVENDER ALMOND MYLK

Creates just under 1 litre

INGREDIENTS:

1 cup	soaked almonds
3 ½ cups	filtered water
1 tsp	cinnamon
1 tsp	vanilla
2	medjool dates, pitted

pinch	Himalayan salt
1 tsp	cardamom
1 ½ tsp	fresh lavender or
1 tsp	dried or

3-4 drops lavender
food-grade essential oil

HOW TO:

Soak your almonds overnight in filtered water. Add all ingredients into blender and blend on high.

Holistic Lattes

GINGER TURMERIC LATTE

Serves 1

INGREDIENTS:

1 tsp	ground turmeric
1 tsp	ground ginger (or fresh ginger)
1 cup	homemade almond mylk
1 tbsp	coconut butter
pinch	black pepper
¼ tsp	ground cardamom
½ tsp	ground vanilla
½ tsp	ground cinnamon
pinch	Himalayan salt
½ tbsp	honey

HOW TO:

If using a Vitamix, add all ingredients into blender and blend on high for 2 minutes (it will start warming).

With another blender, warm all ingredients except the honey in a saucepan at medium heat for 2 minutes. Once warmed, add ingredients + honey in blender and blend on high for 1 minute.

MATCHA LATTE

INGREDIENTS:

1 ½ cups almond mylk

1 tbsp   coconut butter

½ tbsp   matcha green tea
          powder

1 tsp   vanilla

1 tsp   cinnamon

HOW TO:

Add all ingredients into blender, blend on high
for 1 minute.

Sauces & Dressings

RASPBERRY CHIA JAM

RASPBERRY CHIA JAM

makes 3/4 cup jam

INGREDIENTS:

1 cup raspberries (fresh or frozen)

2 tbsp filtered water

1 tbsp maple syrup

2 tbsp chia seeds

pinch of cinnamon

HOW TO:

Mix the water and chia seeds in a bowl and let it sit in the fridge for 5 minutes. In a blender, combine this mixture with the rest of the ingredients and pulse. Feel free to add extra water if you need.

Heat the mixture in a saucepan over medium heat for 2 minutes. Remove it from the heat, mix and serve or store in the fridge.

CHOCOLATE ORANGE TAHINI SAUCE

makes ½ cup sauce

INGREDIENTS:

2 tbsp   tahini

2 tbsp   raw cacao

2 tbsp   almond mylk

1 tsp   maple syrup

1 tsp   cinnamon

⅛ tsp   orange food-grade essential oil

HOW TO:

Combine the tahini, cacao, maple syrup, cinnamon and Himalayan salt- and stir it until it creates a thick paste. Slowly add in the almond milk and stir until it's a smooth and creamy consistency. Perfect to drizzle on pancakes and desserts!

GLORY BOWL SAUCE

makes 3 servings

INGREDIENTS:

1 ½ tbsp almond butter

1 tsp miso paste

2 inch piece of ginger root

1 garlic clove

1 tbsp tamari

1 tbsp tahini

2 tbsp filtered water

HOW TO:

Add all ingredients into blender, blend on high.

PEANUTTY THAI SAUCE

makes 2 servings

INGREDIENTS:

½ tbsp tahini

1-2 garlic cloves

1 tsp black pepper

1 handful fresh coriander

1 tbsp fresh lime juice

1 ½ tbsp peanut butter

½ tbsp tamari

1 inch piece of ginger

pinch red chili flakes

VEGAN CAESER DRESSING

makes 4-6 servings

INGREDIENTS:

2	garlic cloves	1 lemon	juiced & zested
¾ cup	soaked cashews	1 tbsp	apple cider vinegar
½ tbsp	Dijon mustard	2 ½ tbsp	nutritional yeast
3 tbsp	filtered water	1 tsp	black pepper
1 tbsp	olive oil	1 tsp	sea/Himalayan salt
2 medjool dates, pitted			

HOW TO:

Add all ingredients into a blender and blend on high until smooth and creamy.

chloe's COUNTERTOP

GINGER MISO DRESSING

makes ⅓ cup sauce

INGREDIENTS:

2 tbsp	miso paste	1 medjool date, pitted	
1 tbsp	lemon juice	1 tbsp	tahini
1 tbsp	apple cider vinegar	1 inch piece of ginger root	
2 tbsp	olive oil	1 tsp black pepper	

HOW TO:

Add all ingredients into a blender and blend on high.

chloe's
COUNTERTOP

LEMON RANCH DIPPING SAUCE

makes 1 cup of sauce

INGREDIENTS:

1 x 1 lb	organic silken tofu packet		1 tbsp	filtered water
1 lemon	juiced & zested		1 ½ tbsp	apple cider vinegar
3	garlic cloves		1 tsp	onion powder
½ tsp	sea salt		2 tbsp	fresh chives
½ tsp	black pepper		⅓ cup	parsley
			1 tsp	smoked paprika

HOW TO:

Combine all ingredients into a blender and blend on high for 1 minute or until smooth and creamy.

chloe's
COUNTERTOP

ALMOND MACA BUTTER

makes 2 cups of almond butter

INGREDIENTS:

2 cups	almonds
2 tbsp	maca powder
1 tsp	sea salt
1 tsp	cinnamon
1 tbsp	coconut oil

HOW TO:

Add all almonds onto a baking sheet and roast in the oven at 200 degrees for 10 minutes.

Combine almonds and coconut oil in a high-speed blender or food processor and blend on high until creamy, stopping frequently to push the sides down when needed. It will take around 15-20 minutes of this. It's a labor of love that is always worth it.

Once you have reached the creamy consistency, add your sea salt, cinnamon and maca powder and blend on medium.

SALTED CASHEW BUTTER

makes 2 cups of cashew butter

INGREDIENTS:

2 cups	cashews
2 tsp	sea salt
1 tbsp	coconut oil

HOW TO:

Combine cashews and coconut oil in a high-speed blender or food processor and blend on high until creamy, stopping frequently to push the sides down when needed. This will take around 5-10 minutes. Once you have reached the creamy consistency, add your sea salt and blend on medium.

chloe's COUNTERTOP

WALNUT PESTO

INGREDIENTS:

½ cup	olive oil	1 tbsp	nutritional yeast
½ cup	fresh basil leaves	2	garlic cloves
½ cup	organic walnuts, soaked	1 tsp	black pepper
⅓ cup	pine nuts	1 tsp	sea salt
⅓ cup	hemp hearts	1 tbsp	lemon juice

HOW TO:

Blend all ingredients on high until creamy (around 1 minute)

Salads

PINK KALE SALAD

INGREDIENTS:

2 cups	Kale
1	carrot, grated
1	beet, grated
2 tbsp	chopped walnuts
1 tbsp	Almond parmesan

DRESSING:

2 tbsp	dijon
2 tbsp	acv
1 tbsp	olive oil
2	garlic cloves
1	whole lemon
¼	tsp sea salt
¼	tsp black pepper
2 tbsp	tahini
½ tbsp	filtered water
1 tsp	maple syrup

HOW TO:

De-stem kale, wash and tear into bite size pieces. Place in a bowl and massage with 1 tbsp lemon juice + 1 tsp himalayn salt. Add grated carrots and beets. Blend sauce on high until smooth and creamy. Add dressing to salad, and mix well until sauce goes pink from beets. Sprinkle with crushed walnuts and almond parmesan.

CHEEZY GREENS

serves 4

INGREDIENTS:

1   large bunch of kale

1 cup   of spinach

½ cup   arugula

1 tbsp   lemon juice

1 tsp   himalayn salt

CHEEZY SAUCE:

1 cup   cashews

4   garlic cloves

2 tbsp   lemon juice

2 tbsp   nutritional yeast

1 tsp   himalayan salt

½ cup   water

HOW TO:

De-stem kale, wash and tear into bite size pieces.

Place kale in a bowl, add lemon juice and salt and massage for 2 minutes.

Add spinach and arugula into the bowl and mix.

Add all sauce ingredients into a blender, blend on high for 1 minute (until smooth and creamy).

Pour into salad bowl, mix with hands to ensure proper dressing.

Serve topped with pumpkin seeds, sprouts or sauerkraut

chloe's COUNTERTOP

CLASSIC KALE

serves 3-4

INGREDIENTS:

1 head   green kale

1 tbsp   olive oil

2 tbsp   lemon juice

1 tsp   sea salt

HOW TO:

De-stem your kale leaves

Wash the leaves and rip into bite-size pieces

Add olive oil, lemon juice and sea salt and use your (clean) hands to massage the leaves with the oil/ lemon juice mix for around 2-5 minutes. Massaging the kale will help to break down the cellulose walls and make the leaves better at absorbing dressing and easier to digest (not to mention delicious!)

*add glory bowl dressing to massaged kale or desired dressing.

Soups

CREAMY CAULIFLOWER COCONUT SOUP

serves 4-6

INGREDIENTS:

1 head	cauliflower
1	yellow onion
1 can	coconut milk, full-fat
1 ½ cups	filtered water OR vegetable broth
1 tbsp	coconut oil
1 tbsp	olive oil
1 lemon	juiced

himalayan salt to taste

black pepper to taste

spring onion, chopped (for topping)

HOW TO:

Chop cauliflower into pieces and place in a baking dish dressed in olive oil, salt and pepper. Roast in the oven for about 15 minutes until lightly toasted.

Dice onion and sauté in coconut oil until lightly translucent. Remove cauliflower from oven and add the pot with the onions. Add coconut milk and water/vegetable broth and bring to a boil. Turn down heat, and use a hand blender or transfer to a blender to blend soup into a creamy texture. Season to taste with lemon juice, sea salt and black pepper. Serve in a bowl with green onion and splash of organic extra-virgin olive oil.

CREAMY CURRIED PUMPKIN SOUP

serves 4-6

INGREDIENTS:

1	large pumpkin, chopped
1	large yellow onion, diced
3 cloves	garlic, minced
4 inch	piece of ginger root, minced
1 can	coconut cream (full-fat)
2 ½ cups	filtered water
	himalayan salt
	black pepper
1 tsp	cayenne
½ tbsp	cumin
1 whole	lemon, juiced
2 tbsp	olive oil

HOW TO:

Start by chopping the pumpkin into quarter pieces and placing them on parchment paper on a baking sheet. Roast for 20 minutes at 350 degrees seasoned with a pinch of sea salt, black pepper and olive oil.

In a pot at medium heat, add olive oil and yellow onion and cook for 2 minutes or until translucent. Add the ginger, garlic and spices and continue cooking for another 5 minutes (making sure not to burn the garlic). Once the pumpkin is finished roasting, add it into the pot along with the rest of the ingredients. Cover and turn the heat to low medium and cook down for another 15-20 minutes.

Take the pot off the heat and with a hand-blender, blend the soup until smooth and creamy. Before serving, squeeze lemon juice and top with fresh cilantro or parsley (your choice).

MUSHROOM GINGER MISO SOUP

INGREDIENTS:

1	yellow onion, sliced
2	garlic cloves, minced
2 inch	piece of ginger root, minced
1 ½ cups	mushrooms (brown crimini, shiitake, portobello)
2 tbsp	chickpea miso or organic white miso paste
2 tbsp	organic gluten-free tamari
½	avocado
2 cups	hot water
2	dates (optional)
1 tbsp	dulse flakes
1 tbsp	raw tahini
½ tbsp	coconut oil

HOW TO:

In a saucepan on medium-high heat, sauté onion, garlic and ginger for 2-3 minutes.

Add mushrooms and sauté for another 2-3 minutes.

Take it off the heat, and combine all of the ingredients (including sautéed ingredients) into a blender and blend on high until creamy and smooth

Pour into a large bowl, garnish with suggested toppings

GARNISH:

3	sliced brown crimini mushrooms, marinated in 1 tbsp tamari for 10 minutes
handful	fresh cilantro
1 tbsp	dulse flakes
1 tsp	white sesame seeds

Holistic Makeovers

CURRIED CAULIFLOWER HOT WINGS + LEMON RANCH SAUCE

serves 4-6

inspired by hotforfoodblog.com

INGREDIENTS:

1	Head Cauliflower

BATTER:

½ cup	chickpea flour
¼ cup	gluten-free rice flour
½ cup	almond mylk (unsweetened, no cinnamon)
½ cup	filtered water
2 tsp	onion powder
2 tsp	garlic powder
1 tsp	smoked paprika
2 tsp	cumin & coriander
2 tsp	ground turmeric
1 tsp	black pepper
1 tsp	chilli powder/ cayenne

HOT WING SAUCE:

2 tbsp	coconut oil
¾ tsp	ranks red hot sauce
¼ tsp	cayenne
½ tsp	cumin
1 tbsp	lemon juice

HOW TO:

Preheat your oven to 350 degrees and line your baking sheet with parchment paper. Wash and cut the cauliflower head into bize sized pieces.

Mix all of the ingredients for the batter in a bowl. You are looking for a creamy consistency that is slightly thick but not so thick that it doesn't drip off the spoon, and not too thin that it doesn't stick to the cauliflower. If it is too thick, add some more liquid or vice versa.

Dip each cauliflower piece into the batter and coat completely. Make sure that you let the excess drip off, and then place it onto the baking sheet. Repeat this step with each cauliflower floret.

Bake for 20-25 minutes or until golden brown. You will want to flip the cauliflower pieces over half way through to bake each side and achieve the crispy consistency that mimics a chicken wing.

In the meantime, quickly make your curried hot wing sauce. Melt the coconut oil over a low heat and add the rest of the ingredients, mixing to create a smooth consistency.

Take the cauliflower pieces out of the oven, dip them in the hot wing sauce and place them back on the baking sheet. Place them back in the oven to cook for another 10-15 minutes. Pay attention to how the cauliflower bakes and how long it takes to get crispy. Every oven is different and this recipe varies based on what kitchen I am in.

Serve it in a bowl/basket with a homemade lemon ranch dressing.

HOLISTIC POPCORN

INGREDIENTS:

¼ cup	Organic popcorn kernals
2 tbsp	Coconut oil
1 tsp	Cumin powder
1 tsp	Garlic powder
2 tsp	Sea salt
1 tsp	Cinnamon powder
1 tsp	Chilli powder
2 tsp	raw honey or maple syrup

HOW TO:

Pop the corn kernels in an air popper using the directions provided with the machine or on the stovetop in a saucepan (if in the saucepan add ½ tbsp coconut oil)

Melt the coconut oil while the popcorn is popping and add in your spices and honey. Once popcorn is done popcorn, coat generously with your topping.

chloe's COUNTERTOP

RAW-NUT TACOS

makes 1 cup

INGREDIENTS:

1 cup	raw walnuts
1 tbsp	tamari
⅛ tsp	cayenne
⅛ tsp	paprika
1 tsp	cumin
1 tsp	olive oil

HOW TO:

Place all ingredients into a food processor or blender and pulse to mix. Do not over-blend the mixture; you want to create a ground taco-meat like texture. Use as a topping for salads, dips, or in raw/vegan lettuce wraps and corn tortillas.

chloe's
COUNTERTOP

VEGAN ALFREDO MARINARA

1	cauliflower (florets only)
½ cup	soaked cashews
1 cup	tomato sugo/sauce
2 tsp	sea salt
2 tsp	black pepper
½ tsp	cayenne
1 tsp	chilli powder
1 tsp	turmeric powder
1 tsp	coriander
1 tbsp	lemon juice

fresh parsley to dress

Choice of pasta: fusilli, spaghetti, linguine (go for an organic, gf version if possible such as brown rice pasta or buckwheat)

Optional: nutritional yeast (for more cheezy)

HOW TO:

Steam your cauliflower so that it is partially cooked and soft (around 15 minutes)

Cook your pasta, drain it, rinse it (if it's gluten-free), add a dash of olive oil and leave it in a covered pot.

Place all ingredients into a blender, and blend on high for 2 minutes (you may need to add water depending on how thick it is you can adjust)

Add the blended sauce to your pasta, cover and heat on low if needed. Careful not to burn

Serve with fresh parsley

STUFFED SWEET POTATO

chloe's
COUNTERTOP

STUFFED SWEET POTATO

INGREDIENTS:

1	medium sized sweet potato

coconut butter or ghee

1 cup	mushrooms, sliced
⅓	leek (white), sliced
½	avocado, sliced

Favourite homemade or store bought vegan cheese

Green onion

Cilantro

1 tsp	turmeric
1 tsp	sea salt
1 tsp	black pepper
⅛ tsp	chilli powder or cayenne

HOW TO:

Wash sweet potato and poke holes throughout with a fork (to speed up cooking time). Wrap potato in aluminum foil and bake in the oven for 1 hour at 350 degrees C.

Meanwhile, sautee your leeks and mushrooms in coconut oil along with sea salt, black pepper, turmeric, and chilli (optional)

Once sweet potato is done (test with a fork or just use your hands to feel how firm or squishy it is. Depending on the size of the potato it may take more or less than an hour.

Slice it in half (don't cut all the way through) and layer with your favourite toppings in this sequence:

Coconut oil, mushrooms & leeks, avocado, vegan cheese

GLORY BOWL + GLORY BOWL SAUCE

serves 2-3

INGREDIENTS:

1/2 cup	quinoa, soaked
2 cups	Classic Kale
	tempeh
	tamari
1	yam/sweet potato
2	beetroots
1	carrot
1	avocado
	sauerkraut
	sprouts

OPTIONAL:

Top with crushed almonds, desiccated coconut and cacao nibs for some extra crunch"

HOW TO:

This is one of those amazing assemble bowls. Meaning, you prepare several components and then combine to make a bowl of nourishment. Start by soaking and then cooking your quinoa: rinse and then soak for 3+ hours in filtered water. Drain and then cook ½ cup of quinoa + 1 cup of water.

Marinate tempeh in 2 tbsp tamari for 1+ hr. Bake or fry for 10 minutes.

Dice the yam/sweet potato and beetroot into small pieces and bake in the oven at 350 for 15 minutes or until soft

Cut the avocado into pieces or mash it up into a guacamole.

Grate the carrot and beetroot

Assemble: quinoa at the bottom + roasted vegetables + diced tempeh + grated carrot/beetroot + avocado + classic kale + glory bowl sauce + sauerkraut + sprouts

LEMON BEETROOT HUMMUS

makes 2 cups

INGREDIENTS:

2 cups   chickpeas (soaked overnight, cooked) <u>or</u>

2 cans   of chickpeas

3 tbsp   olive oil

¼ cup   water

1 ½ tbsp tahini

2 lemons juiced and zest

1 tsp   cumin

2 garlic cloves

1 beetroot, raw OR roasted

HOW TO:

Combine all ingredients into a blender, blend on high until creamy (about 30 seconds-1 minute)

MUSHROOM RISOTTO + VEGAN PARMESAN CHEESE

chloe's
COUNTERTOP

MUSHROOM RISOTTO +
VEGAN PARMESAN CHEESE

serves 4

INGREDIENTS:

2 cups	mixed mushrooms (brown crimini, shiitake, Portobello, chaneterelles, oyster)
2 cups	organic, gluten-free vegetable stock OR filtered water
1 cup	wild rice blend, soaked
2	garlic cloves, minced
1	leek (white), diced
1 tbsp	olive oil
½ tbsp	coconut oil
1 tbsp	lemon juice
2 tbsp	almond mylk (unsweetened, no cinnamon)
2 tsp	cumin
1 tsp	turmeric
1 tsp	black pepper
2 tsp	sea salt

handful of spinach

HOW TO:

In a saucepan on medium heat, add your olive and coconut oil and add the leeks. Sautee until translucent (around 2 minutes) and add mushrooms and garlic. Turn heat down slightly, careful to not burn the garlic. After the mushrooms begin to release their natural oil, add the cumin, turmeric and black pepper and continue cooking. Add the wild rice, vegetable stock, turn the heat to low and cover. Cook for 30-40 minutes, stirring occasionally. Watch it, and add more water or vegetable stock if needed.

5 minutes before serving, add the 2 tbsp of almond mylk and stir to coat. Take the risotto off the heat, add the lemon juice and spinach and mix it in. Serve sprinkled with vegan parmesan.

chloe's
COUNTERTOP

VEGAN PARMESAN CHEESE

Makes 1/3 cup of cheese

INGREDIENTS:

½ tsp   garlic powder

¼ tsp   turmeric

½ tsp   sea salt

2 tbsp   nutritional yeast

¼ cup   roasted almonds

HOW TO:

In a coffee grinder or food processor, combine all ingredients and pulse lightly into a parmesan texture

MANGO CHICKPEA COCONUT CURRY

serves 4-6

INGREDIENTS:

1 ½   cups of dried chickpeas (soaked overnight, cooked) or 1 can chickpeas

1 cup   fresh mango, diced

1 can   full-fat coconut mylk

2   garlic cloves

1   yellow onion

1   jalapeno

1 tbsp   ground cumin

handful fresh coriander

1 tsp   black pepper

¼ tsp   cardamom

⅛ tsp   cinnamon

2 inch piece of ginger root

½ tbsp   turmeric

2 tsp   sea salt

1 cup   green or red lentils (soaked overnight, sprouted)

1 tbsp   coconut oil

handful of spinach

1   sweet potato, diced into small pieces

HOW TO:

In a large saucepan, add your coconut oil and heat it on medium heat. Add the onion, and sautee for 2 minutes until translucent. Add the ginger, garlic, jalapeno and your spices and cook for 5 minutes. Add the sweet potato and cook on medium-low for 5 minutes. Add the chickpeas, lentils, mango, coconut mylk, and fresh coriander and cover to cook for 25-30 minutes. Before serving, add the fresh spinach and serve either on it's own or with quinoa/wild rice and top with fresh coriander.

chloe's
COUNTERTOP

VEGAN TERIYAKI STIR FRY + BLACK BEAN NOODLES + THAI PEANUTTY SAUCE

chloe's
COUNTERTOP

VEGAN TERIYAKI STIR FRY + BLACK BEAN NOODLES + THAI PEANUTTY SAUCE

serves 3

INGREDIENTS:

5-6	brown crimini mushrooms, sliced
½	yellow onion, diced
2	carrots, diced
1 cup	chickpeas (soaked overnight, cooked)
handful of kale/spinach	
1 head	broccoli, chopped (including broccoli stem)
handful of chard	
tempeh	
1 tbsp	tamari
seasonal vegetables	
1 tbsp	coconut oil
1 tsp	turmeric
1 tbsp	green onion, diced
½ tbsp	sesame seeds
3	servings of black bean paleo noodles

HOW TO:

In a saucepan, combine coconut oil and onion. Sautee for 5 minutes or until onion is translucent. Add the turmeric and mushrooms and cook down for 5 minutes. Add the rest of the vegetables, except the greens (spinach/kale/chard).

Cook for 5 minutes, covered.

In the meantime, bake or fry your tempeh in tamari

Cook your black bean noodles according to the instructions (cooks for 2-5 minutes, strain and run under cold water, place in a covered pot with some olive oil to avoid sticking together)—you can also use wild rice, buckwheat soba noodles or quinoa.

Add 2-3 tbsp of thai peanutty sauce (find recipe in sauces & dressings), mix and serve over a bed of noodles. Top with green onion, sesame seeds and fresh coriander

THE BEST GUACAMOLE

INGREDIENTS:

5	ripe avocados
¼	red onion, minced
1	garlic clove, minced
2	limes (juiced & zested)
1 tsp	sea salt
1 tsp	black pepper
1	jalapeno, minced
1	handful fresh cilantro
	baby bell peppers, minced
½ cup	cherry tomatoes, chopped
¼ tsp	cumin seeds

HOW TO:

To start, in a bowl or pestle and mortar- add your garlic, onion, cilantro, jalapeno, cumin seeds, lime juice and lime zest and grind it down for around 2-5 minutes. The idea is to really blend all of the ingredients together, break the cell-wall down and release the essential oils and qualities of each ingredient. Once you have finished grinding- add your 5 ripe avocados one by one. With a fork, mash each avocado into the pre-made mixture and mix well to combine all of the flavours. It's up to you on how mashed or chunky you would like it.

Serve this delicious guacamole with your favourite corn chips, on toast (think: avocado toast) or in your favourite bowl of nourishment (think: Glory Bowl).

Enjoy!

TIP:

See the next page for info on how to choose the perfect avocado!

HOW TO CHOOSE THE PERFECT AVOCADO:

I have a few ways of knowing which avocados I want. The first thing is to plan ahead and know when you will be consuming the avocados. If it won't be for a few days, it's ok to get a less ripe (greener and harder) avocado and place it in a paper bag overnight before you will be using them. If you are using them day of, the idea is to choose avocados that are a darker colour (more black than green), feel soft to touch but not overly soft or moushy.

If you direct your attention to the area where the outer pit is- pushing down on that area will give you a good indication of the level of ripeness. Also, the last and best way to check is to remove this pit and have a small window into what is going on underneath the skin. If you see bright/light green and clean- it's good to go. If it looks brown and slightly moldy- chances are, it's over-ripe and a "bad egg".

chloe's
COUNTERTOP

PARTY TIME VEGAN SPINACH ARTICHOKE DIP serves 8-10

INGREDIENTS:

2 bags	(4 cups) of frozen or fresh spinach
2 cans	artichoke hearts, quartered
1 Tofutti	(better than cream cheese) 277g packed
¾ cup	unsweetened almond mylk
3-4 tbsp	nutritional yeast
2 tsp	sea salt
2 tsp	black pepper
2 tbsp	olive oil
1	yellow onion, diced
4	garlic cloves, minced
1 ½	cup cashews, soaked
pinch	cayenne
½ tbsp	coconut oil

small handful fresh basil or ¼ tsp dried basil

HOW TO:

Start by heating onion and garlic in coconut oil in a pan.

Sautee for 3 minutes.

Combine all ingredients (except spinach and artichoke) into a high-speed blender or food processor and blend until smooth and creamy In a large pan or pot- combine the creamy mixture, artichokes and spinach and heat for 5-10 minutes on medium, stirring to ensure no burning- to heat the spinach. Make sure the mixture is properly heated.

Place in a preheated oven and cook on broil for 5-8 minutes to lightly brown. Make sure not to burn.

Serve with organic corn tortilla chips, sourdough, crackers or cut up vegetables (carrots, broccoli, cucumber)

chloe's COUNTERTOP

Desserts

PINEAPPLE MATCHA CHEEZECAKE

PINEAPPLE MATCHA CHEEZECAKE

makes 1 cake – 16 servings

BASE:

1 cup	almonds
½ cup	hazelnuts/almonds/ walnuts
⅛ tsp	sea salt
¼ tsp	cinnamon
6	pitted dates

FILLING:

4 cups	fresh pineapple
2 cups	cashews
¼ tsp	sea salt
8	drops of lemon essentail oil
1	lemon, juiced and zested
¾ cup	honey
¾ cup	coconut oil
1 tsp	cinnamon

MATCHA:

½ filling +

1 ½ tsp   matcha powder

HOW TO:

Start by soaking your cashews for the filling in filtered water for 3 hours (or overnight).

Combine all base ingredients into a food processor or blender and pulse until partially blended and sticks together. Roll into a ball, and transfer into a spring-form pan. Gently push down with your fingers until entire bottom of pan is covered. Place in a freezer while you make the filling to solidify.

Combine all filling ingredients into a blender, blend on high for 1-2 minutes until creamy- use the tamper if needed. Gently pour ½ filling into spring-form pan, allow it to set in the freezer (10-15 minutes) while you make the matcha filling. Place matcha powder into blender along with second ½ of the filling. Blend on high until well combined (filling should be a light green in colour). Pour second half of filling into spring-form pan in various spots. With a toothpick or fork, carefully draw figure eights throughout filling to create a marble-like design. Place in freezer and leave for at least 5-6 hours. Allow cake to thaw for 2 hours in the fridge before serving.

RASPBERRY STRAWBERRY SWIRL CHEEZE CAKE

RASPBERRY STRAWBERRY SWIRL CHEEZE CAKE

makes 1 cake – 12-16 servings

BASE:

½ cup	pecans
¾ cup	rolled oats
1 cup	medjool dates
¼ cup	walnuts
1 tsp	sea salt

FILLING:

2 cups	cashews, soaked
1 can	coconut cream
¼ cup	maple syrup or honey
1 lemon	juiced and zested
5 drops	lemon essential oil

RASPBERRY SWIRL:

1 cup	raspberries
½ cup	strawberries
1 tbsp	honey or maple syrup
1 tbsp	coconut mylk

HOW TO:

Start by soaking your cashews for the filling in filtered water for 3 hours (or overnight).

Combine all base ingredients into a food processor or blender and pulse until partially blended and sticks together. Roll into a ball, and transfer into a spring-form pan. Gently push down with your fingers until entire bottom of pan is covered. Place in a freezer while you make the filling to solidify.

Combine all filling ingredients into a blender, blend on high for 1-2 minutes until creamy- use the tamper if needed. Gently pour filling into spring-form pan, allow it to set in the freezer (10-15 minutes) while you make the raspberry strawberry filling. Place raspberry strawberry ingredients into blender. Blend on high until well combined. Pour raspberry swirl into spring-form pan in various spots. With a toothpick or fork, carefully draw figure eights throughout filling to create a marble-like design. Place in freezer and leave for at least 5-6 hours. Allow cake to thaw for 2 hours in the fridge before serving.

RAW MACA BROWNIES

makes 12 brownies

INGREDIENTS:

2 ½ cups dates, pitted

1 cup raw cacao powder

2 tbsp maca powder

1 cup walnuts

1 cup cashews

¼ tsp himalayan salt

1 tsp cinnamon

HOW TO:

Place nuts into food processor or blender, blend until nuts are finely ground. Add dates, cacao powder, maca, cinnamon and himalayan salt and blend until ingredients combine to make a "dough". Press dough into a pan lined with parchment paper. Place in the freezer for 20-30 minutes or in the fridge for 2-3 hours. Lasts in the freezer for 6+ months or the fridge for 3 weeks. Optional: top with crushed almonds to make them chunky.

chloe's COUNTERTOP

CHILLI CHOCOLATE PUDDING

serves 2–3

INGREDIENTS:

3	avocados
¾ cup	cacao powder
1 tsp	vanilla
1 tsp	cinnamon
1 tsp	cayenne
1 cup	dates, pitted and soaked for 15 minutes
½ cup	water

OPTIONAL:

1 tbsp maple syrup

HOW TO:

Place dates and water in a blender and process on medium for 1 minute. Add the avocado, cacao powder, cinnamon, cayenne and vanilla and process until creamy. Use the tamper to scrape the sides if needed. Serve in a bowl

chloe's
COUNTERTOP

SPICED NUT STUFFED DATES

makes 12

INGREDIENTS:

12	medjool dates, pitted
4 tbsp	almond butter
2 tsp	sea salt
2 tsp	cinnamon
¼ tsp	cardamom
⅛ tsp	black pepper

HOW TO:

Pit all of your dates and split the almond butter proportionately into each date (stuff each date pocket with almond butter). In a separate bowl, mix the spices and sea salt together and then sprinkle over each date. Optional: place in the freezer and keep them on hand for when you need a quick energizing pick-me-up.

chloe's COUNTERTOP

THE LAST WORD

THERE ARE MANY THINGS THAT I WISH FOR YOU FROM THIS BOOK.

I wish for you to find peace in your body.

I wish for you to find silence in your mind.

And I wish for you to find joy in your life.

Like everything that I have created, there is a lot of love, heart and soul that has gone into this book and I hope that the energy is transferred into your hands in some way. We all have ways of communicating our magic, and passing on our wisdom. For me, nothing is more mystical than the moments that I have here with you on the page. There is something that happens when you allow yourself to truly be and create, without the restrictions of your mind's noise. The same goes for a life with nourishing food, supportive love and energizing movement.

We can all get caught up in the busyness and distraction of life. It can happen so quickly. That is what makes us human. There is always the opportunity, though, to witness yourself fall out of alignment and go into reaction. Reactions are about how you feel, what you think, what others think and what may or may not have happened. When you take a step back and allow yourself to observe this, instead of taking part in it; that is when you are offering yourself the opportunity to live a life of light. We all have the chance to do this, no matter who we are and what our story is.

The next time you feel inclined to judge yourself for how you look in those jeans, how that shirt fits you, or the way that your body has bloated- choose to think of love. Think of how stoked you are to wear an epic pair of jeans and how grateful you feel to have legs, arms, fingers and toes. Rather than falling into a pattern of judgment and comparison, choose a path of love and compassion. Take yourself back through Living in Light and be reminded of the simple and beautiful things in life that are worth living for. Use Chloe's Life Plan as your guide, and truly allow yourself to live in light.

I love you.

Chloe

Chloe Elgar is a Holistic Nutritionist, speaker, writer, self-taught food photographer and natural food chef living in Vancouver and Seattle. Chloe works with clients through her 1 on 1, Living True Mentorship, as well as with groups to bring awareness and inspire conversation around body image, intuitive eating and the psychology of eating. Chloe works with women specifically with eating disorders and destructive relationships with food, anxiety and their bodies. Her workshops involve the concepts of intuitive eating, intuitive cooking and conscious living.

Elgar completed her Bachelors (BA) majoring in Psychology and minoring in English Literature at the University of British Columbia in Vancouver. Since then, Chloe attended the Institute of Holistic Nutrition in Vancouver, attaining her certification as a Certified Nutritional Practitioner (CNP). Her work is inspired through her experiences with eating disorders, depression and anxiety.